LEADING SCHOOLS
SCHOOLS
of DIVERSITY

Rural • Suburban • Urban

LEADING
SCHOOLS
of DIVERSITY

Rural • Suburban • Urban

BUILDING SCHOOLS OF COLLABORATION, UNDERSTANDING AND COOPERATION

Dr. Kevin Caress • Wilmer Cooper • Dr. Eugene White

Leading Schools of Diversity

Dr. Kevin Caress, Wilmer Cooper, Dr. Eugene White

ISBN-13: 9780979589973
ISBN-10: 0979589975

Library of Congress Cataloging in Publication Data in Progress.

This book is manufactured in the United States of America.

Power Publishing
13680 N. Duncan Drive
Camby, IN 46113
(317) 347-1051
www.powerpublishinginc.com

Editor: Janet Schwind
Cover Design: Parada Design

CONTENTS

Chapter 1

Communications
and Media Relations

Rural Perspective

As a classroom teacher, administrator, central office secretary, custodian, bus driver, cafeteria worker or student, the fact that you spend a minimum of six hours per day at the school or place of business is reason enough to become familiar with a culture different from your own. Have you noticed the routine demonstrated by your office mate who prays before eating lunch? Have you sensed the frustration exhibited by the lady next door when the entire office is required to salute the flag each Monday morning? How do you feel at break time when one of the guys from personnel shares a joke that really smacks of prejudice?

The school and office are more diverse than ever before. There are now people of various colors and religions, and the importance of these differences is a constant topic at the workplace. There are even men and women who oppose the traditional roles of family membership. The people of today's workplace are diverse; their values are different and their beliefs are different. Diversity is defined as a conscious practice to recognize and understand the value of the characteristics and beliefs of individuals from a wide range of ethnic and racial backgrounds, gender, age language, exceptionality, religion, class, and national origin. Included in this definition is the ability or knowledge of how to communicate with individuals who possess the qualities and conditions that are outside my group (LAS, 2004).

While the purpose of this chapter is to outline the steps necessary for effective communication and media relations, the initial step must be clearly articulated and understood. For starters, you must accept that diversity is not just a buzz word circulating in urban educational centers; diversity is a reality in all school settings.

According to the National Center for Education Statistics (NCES), in

2004, 43 percent of public school students were considered to be part of a racial or ethnic minority group, up from 22 percent in 1972. In comparison, the percentage of public school students who were White decreased from 78 to 57 percent. The minority increase was largely because of the growth in the proportion of students who were Hispanic, up from 6 percent in 1972 to 19 percent in 2004. The proportion of students who are African American or members of other minority groups increased less over this period than the proportion who were Hispanic. Hispanic enrollment surpassed that of African American for the first time in 2002. In the West, beginning in 2003, minority public school enrollment exceeded Caucasian enrollment (2006, p. 5).

The number of students of color, including Hispanic students, increases each year, as government-sponsored studies and data collection efforts such as the Census tells us (NCES, 2005, 2006; U.S. Census, 2003). Another quickly growing segment of the student body, estimated to be about 17 percent in 1999, speaks a native language other than English (NCES, 2003a). During the same year, about 8 percent of children were estimated to receive English language services in school (NCES, 2003a). These numbers are also certainly higher by now.

In contrast to students, about 90 percent of teachers in the United States are White (National Education Association [NEA], 2003). Throw into this mix the fact that 79 percent of teachers are female (NEA, 2003), and one can easily see the homogeneity of much of the teacher workforce. The predilection of American schools to be segregated by race and economic class creates the additional tendency for a growing number of schools to be characterized by White adults working almost exclusively with children of color (Donato, Menchaca, & Valencia, 1991; NCES, 2004, 2005; NEA, 2003; Tatum, 1999; Trueba, 1998). Indeed, in 2005, the Pew Hispanic Center reported that "Hispanic teens are more likely than Blacks and Whites to attend public high schools that have the most students, the highest concentration of poor students and highest student-teacher ratios" (Pew, 2005). It is possible for Hispanic and African American students in the United States to spend their entire school careers without meeting a single teacher of color.

To work effectively with the heterogeneous population (diversity) found in schools, educators must feel comfortable and understand the cultural setting in which the school is located, help students become aware of cultural differences and inequalities throughout the world, and help students affirm cultural differences while realizing similarities in cultures (Gollnick and Chin, 2006).

Educators will discover that students from the same culture will even show individual differences; they will bring into the classroom different historical backgrounds, religious beliefs, and everyday experiences that greatly affect behavior. For some students, the culture of the school itself will be reflected in them; for others, the differences between the home and school culture will create dissonance if the educator does not integrate cultural pluralism into the curriculum to create a supportive learning environment within the classroom. Failure to understand cultural factors, in addition to physical and intellectual factors, impacts learning and behavior, and makes it almost impossible to lead the school toward cultural responsiveness (Gollnick and Chin, 2006).

Rural schools share the common problems of communication with urban schools: methodology, cost, feedback, etc., but rural schools are also unique in that the school is traditionally the largest employer, the most popular topic of conversation, and the strongest organization within the community. With these factors in mind, one can understand a common stereotype of rural communication: one story told will be shared frequently and modified greatly. In a rural school classroom where the student-teacher ratio is generally 1 to 15 or fewer, getting the message to everyone is less daunting when compared to urban schools, in which the ratio will exceed 1 to 15 and there will be several classrooms per grade. Rural schools may also have two grade levels within the same classroom (Pre-K and kindergarten, first and second, third and fourth, etc.). As a result of the size, communication strategies in rural schools are streamlined, yet very important. Rural school communication begins with curriculum; what is taught is more important than methodology. Second, rural school communication demands equity. The third component of rural school communication is student/teacher relationships, and the final component of rural school communications is student engagement.

The curriculum focuses on the knowledge and skills identified by all the school stakeholders as essential for developing and maintaining a quality life. Rural school parental involvement in the curriculum is dependent upon three factors: parental role construction (the parent's beliefs about the actions they should undertake for and with their children or what parents believe they should do to guide the education of their children), a sense of self efficacy, and perception of how parental involvement is accepted (Hoover-Dempsey and Sandler, 1995).

Keep in mind that from the rural school perspective, values are traditional. Discipline, for example, in school refers to classroom management and respect for authority. Many parents who get involved do so as a means of assisting the teacher. Generally rural parents accept the teacher as the authority and demand that students respect this as well.

From the rural school perspective, the key role of the teacher, as it applies to communication, is to share information. When the classroom teacher (the authority) sends a message that says, "I need help or come join the celebration," then the response of the parent may reflect any of the three factors stated previously by Hoover-Dempsey and Sandler.

The level of these factors varies according to socio-economic conditions. Higher income families traditionally have a higher level of parental involvement, a greater sense of self-efficacy, and a more positive perception of parental involvement than lower income families; this same trend crosses racial/cultural boundaries. These factors have a greater significance in Caucasian parents than African American and Hispanic parents. The following is a list of ways to increase parental role construction, provide a greater sense of self-efficacy, and improve the perception of parental involvement for all parents regardless of race, ethnicity, or culture:

- Make sure the school attitude is positive. Refrain from condescending tones and gestures, and recognize that terms such as "dysfunctional family" may not be acceptable.

- Reach out to parents to form a collaborative partnership (Gollnick & Chin 2006).

- Actively respond to parental concerns (Manning & Baruth, 2000).

- Foster the academic and social development of all students by developing effective classroom management skills.

- Maximize the inclusion of diverse cultures in the classroom environment, textbooks, instruction and community resources.

- Be flexible yet consistent with discipline practices that are designed to help students assume responsibility for their actions.

- Affirm the students' language code while assisting students with articulation of standard English.

- Develop and utilize assessment tools to focus on strengths and weaknesses as evaluation of instructional effectiveness.

- Actively encourage parent/teacher partnerships with diverse parents by making the first contact a positive one.

  o Remember that African American and Hispanic parents (just like Caucasian parents) may still harbor bad memories of school experiences.

  o Schools must make an effort to promote the strengths of all students as a way of removing negative thoughts held by parents.

- Don't be hypocritical.

  o If you say positive things during the conference with parents, then make sure they are reflected on the grade card.

- Make use of community resources.

  o Many parents have strong ties to church and civic organizations; use them as a resource (Kuykendall, 1988).

Media Relations

The final component for this section, which addresses communication, is media relations. The absence of television stations in rural areas does not make communication insurmountable. Newspaper and radio coverage in rural schools is a very acceptable type of communication; both of these venues are very active in their support of extra-curricular activities.

The use of radio and newspaper to communicate all activities as well as instruction must be expanded.

The fastest growing media relations tool in rural schools is electronic communication. Within the state of Oklahoma, for example, all administrative communications between the State Department of Education and the local educational agency (school) is electronic; state law requires the placement of all agendas for school board meetings on the school district website. Emails have almost entirely replaced the traditional mail delivery (snail mail).

Electronic communication is also very effective in communicating with parents. I presently serve as the superintendent in a rural school district. With a population fewer than 500 students, cost effective, efficient, reliable, and fast communication is a high priority. The ability to share information with parents is critical; daily lesson plans, homework assignments, grades, report cards, standardized assessment scores, and announcements are all communicated electronically. From the leisure of home or while working at the office, parents have the opportunity to access student information quickly and reliably.

As popular and reliable as electronic communication has become, it does not replace the traditional newspaper and radio. These tools may sometimes suffer a negative perception, but when used properly, both can carry a positive message while probing and seeking accurate information. The local administrator must take advantage of the ability of newspaper and radio to carry positive as well as negative messages. Staying ahead by contacting radio stations and newspapers to share positive information to encourage them to become involved during high times is an effective way to maintain good media relations.

Suburban Perspective

Leaders must be consummate relationship builders with diverse people and groups – especially with people different than themselves.

— Michael Fullan, *Leading in a Culture of Change*

Communications

Building Relationships

The ultimate goal of every educational leader is to make change happen–specifically, change that constantly improves all aspects of the school setting so that, ultimately, every student achieves his highest potential. The key words here are "every student." The most effective leaders in diverse school settings exemplify relationship building and they do it daily among all members of their diverse populations. In other words, you can't successfully lead in a diverse environment without first getting to know intimately all your constituents and all about their unique qualities. This is the first requirement for educational leaders who truly want to make a difference in districts with diverse populations. You need to know all you can about all of these groups on an intimate level.

Practical Applications

Connect With the Key Players

In almost every community with diverse populations, regardless of the size of the community, there are established individuals who arise as leaders of their sub-group, serving as a voice for their fellow minority members in the community. The educational leader who establishes a supportive and open relationship with those leaders of their individual community sub-groups represented in his/her school district will better know and understand the specific needs and overall cultural differences that must be considered to most effectively meet the educational needs of all students.

The effective educational leader of a diverse suburban community should involve those sub-group leaders in the planning process of the school corporation. This involvement may be at the School Board level by either their being a member of the School Board or by their assignment to committee planning groups at the district or school levels. The important thing is that this group of leaders needs to be tapped by educational leadership as a vital source for planning educational change in the community. If such leaders are omitted from the planning process, school leaders run the risk of merely maintaining a status quo school district when it comes to facing the challenges that a diverse population presents. Leaders who want to move a community closer to meeting their educational goals need to consider that "creative ideas and novel solutions are often generated when the status quo is disrupted" (Fullan, 2001).

Historically, school leaders have assumed they knew best what their students and parents needed in the area of educational programming. This single sourced focus is not sufficient for leaders in diverse communities today. All sub-groups need a voice and the effective educational leader will seek out and heed those voices as they plan the districts next steps.

Language Barriers

Despite the fact that the target language of instruction in the U.S. is English, many issues associated with the education of a diverse student population center around the question of overcoming language barriers. This is true with not only students who are overcoming these barriers, but also with the adult/parent population. If a school district's English as a New Language (ENL) program is to be successful, the district's leadership must be able to effectively communicate (regardless of the language barriers) with all of its constituents.

This is a difficult task for communities made up of multiple sub-groups that speak multiple languages, but regardless of the number of languages used, how the school leader addresses this issue is critical for educational success in a diverse community. Short of a school leader becoming bilingual (or in many communities, he/she would have to become multilingual), the key for the educational leader is to develop a plan and provide resources for overcoming any barrier created by language. In many cases, parents are still using their native language or a variation of it, at home with their children. It is the job of the educational leader to provide the most effective means of getting vital school-related information to parents in any understandable form. In many cases, it will require translation and follow-up by school personnel. This is the only way vital communication of school to home information can truly impact learning for the students in a sub-group. School leaders need to know that parents are informed, and that will ensure that both school and home are working together toward the same goal—helping the child succeed.

Classroom Connections

Most school leaders today are hard pressed to spend much time inside a classroom in their school district. If they are to truly become knowledgeable of the issues faced by students as well as teachers, it is requisite that they make the commitment to visit classrooms and engage with students who make up their diverse suburban school community. Although it may seem more difficult to receive a lot of meaningful feedback from elementary-aged students, many middle level and high school level students are very capable of sharing their thoughts and feelings. A school leader might go so far as to adopt a class and set a regular scheduled visitation to that group of students in which he/she has established dialogue. By working through a school counselor, specific interviews could be set up with selected students on a regular basis with school leaders. Whatever means is employed to connect with students, it is important that the school leader be a good listener and that he/she respect the views of these students. Very often their input and ideas on solving educational problems are more clear and concise than the best research in the field. They are especially attuned to what the real issues of their learning may be and are often very open to sharing their views. We must not forget that by understanding their views, we can gain new insight into how we can improve their opportunities for learning.

Listed below are some discussion questions that could be used by school leaders who engage in student discussions to help in better understanding their challenges in the classroom:

1) What language do you use with your family?

2) When at home and you are studying, who helps you if you have trouble completing or understanding your homework?

3) Do your parents speak English?

4) What are the greatest problems you have in becoming better at learning English?

5) Do you have a quiet place to study and do homework at home? Where do you study?

6) Do you study with your peers who are fellow members of your native language group or with native English speakers?

7) Do your parents think it is important for you to become fluent in English?

8) What would you like to see done at school to help you learn English faster and more effectively?

Advocacy in the Community

The effective educational leader in suburban communities with diverse populations may be required to become an advocate for these students among the non-school community members. Presentations to local service organizations and clubs may be the forum where such advocacy occurs. It is not unusual in some communities for the non-school community to form biased views of a sub-group with which they are not familiar. These views may paint broad racial or ethnic generalities over all members of a particular sub-group in a community and create inaccurate portraits of students who may be members of that particular group of people. This may be especially true in communities where a sudden influx of a sub-group has significantly changed the face of a community almost over-night. Perceptions of those sub-groups can lead to misinformation and a general ground swell of negative feelings toward those newcomers to the community. It is in communities experiencing this kind of change that educational leaders need to become a bridge builder, encouraging accep-tance and understanding of these sub-groups into the community, with the education of the public as their main goal in that process. The moral obligation of educating all who enter the school doors must be explained and shared with those who see such change in a community as a negative thing. Perhaps a reminder of the words of Thomas Jefferson on the requisite elements of a republic would be appropriate to share when you speak at the next Rotary meeting. He said, "I have indeed two great measures at heart, without which no republic can maintain itself in strength. 1.) That of general education, to enable *every man* to judge for himself what will secure or endanger his freedom. 2.) To divide every county into hundreds, of such size that *all* the children of each will be within reach of a central school in it" (Thomas Jefferson to John Tyler, 1810 ME 12:93). He also stressed that education for the masses was not to be a function of means. Writing to M. Correa de Serra in 1817, he penned these words: "The object of my education bill was to bring into action that mass of talents which lies buried in poverty in every country for want of the means of development, and thus give activity to a mass of minds which in proportion of our population shall be the double or treble of what it is in most countries" (Thomas Jefferson to M. Correa de Serra, 1817 ME 15:156).

Besides the historical principles of public education's change to educate all who enter our doors, it is important to remind our community members that regardless of a child's parents' origins or legal status as a citizen, the courts have not allowed us to discriminate when it come to allowing for the opportunity to be educated [See Plyler v. Doe, 457 U.S. 202 (1982)]. It is our legal and moral responsibility to provide that opportunity for every child who crosses the thresholds of learning institutions.

Media Relations

The most critical factor for the educational leader to remember when dealing with the media is that he/she needs to communicate the message that they want stressed. For example, when the media questions the progress, or lack of it, in meeting districtwide student achievement goals, and then make sure to also include data showing how much individual progress students have made toward their achievement goals. Educational leaders need to remember that the best responses to a reporter's probing, story-seeking questions are those responses that also report the positive things that are occurring in the school community. Don't allow their questions to limit your answers or put you on the defensive.

Addressing the Diversity Questions

Besides providing the positive message you want to convey to the media, it is very important for educational leaders to continue the role of advocate for the diverse sub-groups of your suburban school district. Frequently, the media has a tendency to oversimplify the reasons a particular school district is not performing as well as they are expected to perform. They may suggest that a particular sub-group is holding the district achievement levels down, and such a single group focus brings into question the value of that sub-group in the community. It is the educational leader's job to ensure that any one sub-group of students are not devalued or seen as a district liability in achieving school improvement goals.

How the educational leader defends the sub-groups in his/her district to the media should be centered on providing the media with details and firsthand views of the programmatic offerings that are assisting these students in increasing their achievement levels. When the media raises questions about the effectiveness of the districts' efforts to improve the academic performance of a specific sub-group, the media should be invited to come into your schools to see for themselves. You might recommend they do a feature article on a specific program that addresses a particular sub-group in the schools. Examples of programs that might be highlighted are ENL services, special needs programs, after school tutoring, technology assisted learning programs, remediation classes, and grant supported initiatives such as Title I or Title III. In summation, open the doors for the media to see firsthand the dedicated personnel and the focused students among these sub-groups who are benefiting from school programs. It is, after all, the number-one job of the leader to educate, and one major vehicle to educate the community is through the media.

Urban Perspective

> If we are to achieve a richer culture, rich in contrasting values, we must recognize the whole gamut of human potentialities and so weave a less arbitrary social fabric, one in which each diverse human gift will find a fitting place.
>
> — Margaret Mead

Caring Must be Communicated

Teachers, administrators and support staff in urban schools must come to realize one fundamental fact about effectively working with most urban children. "The children don't care how much you know until they know how much you care." I don't know who first made this truism, but I know that he or she had to be an urban educator. Many urban students center their first reactions toward teachers and other school people based on how you treat them. They want you to care enough to make them important to you. To communicate effectively, you must talk *to* them and not *at* them. A simple example of this is the teacher who greets his students on the first day, saying, "My name is Mr. Teacher and you will learn math from me because it is important to your future. You won't make it if you can't do it. Now let's get busy. Open your books to page . . ." That teacher is talking *at* students. He isn't saying anything wrong, but he is saying it the wrong way. This might be okay in suburbia or at boarding schools, but for urban students a better approach, which demonstrates caring, would be: "Hello, my name is Mr. Teacher and I am going to teach you math, but before we talk about that, I want to tell you some things about me and I want you to share the same information with me . . . I have been teaching for ten years, I am married and have two children. As a matter of fact my first child,

Tony, is starting first grade this year. He was very nervous about going to school the first day . . . Now tell me something about each of you ... your names, brothers, sisters, things you like, do you like math and were you afraid to go to school your first day?"

Now, the teacher in example one will start teaching and might give some homework, but with urban children he won't have the best start. The teacher in the second example will not teach any math the first day, but he will communicate that he cares enough to share himself with them. Weeks or months later, one of the students will ask him how Tony is doing in school. Simple communications like greeting students each day, letting them know you missed them when they were out, are so important.

When I was the superintendent of a small suburban school district, I made it a point to get out and welcome students back to school each year. In this district about 40 percent of the students were on free and/or reduced priced lunch and about 25 percent of them were African American. I found one observation to be consistent year after year. I would ask my middle income to upper income white students a simple question: "How is your new school year going?" They would commonly tell me how glad they were to be back in school and that they enjoyed their new schedule or the new math or new activity. However, when I asked lower income African American students the question, "How is your school year going?" they would consistently reply that they liked their new teacher or that their new teacher was pretty or nice, or mean, or fun, etc. They overwhelmingly related from the person, not the books or class schedule or math, etc. They wanted their new teacher to like them or love them. They were looking for that personal connection. That is the critical link for effectively communicating with urban students, poor students and I believe, all students.

Leading and teaching in an urban setting is a contact sport or endeavor. The "caring contact" doesn't have to be hugs or physical contacts, but it must convey the message of caring. Too many urban children are impacted by poverty, crime, deprivation, mobility and interrupted relationships. They need something or someone to reach out to, and who will reach out to them. Someone who will "show up" every day and be there for them. That is the tacit communication of stability and sameness. It sends a positive message that brings comfort to many. The most valuable communication in the urban school system is person to person.

To effectively communicate with staff, students, parents and others in an urban school setting requires sensitivity to the unique differences among people, but it demands an understanding of the "sameness" or similarities that diverse people share. A simple view of diversity is variety, difference or variance. Difference, however, doesn't mean deficient; it doesn't mean dysfunctional. It means not the same in some way or ways, e.g., skin color, religious beliefs, language, cultural practices, etc. Diversity is seldom a 100 percent difference, and it is those areas or percentages of "sameness" that gives us hope and opportunity for collaboration, understanding and cooperation.

Common Understanding

Urban schools bring staff, students and others from many backgrounds, beliefs, customs, etc. To create a common foundation of expectations, understandings and communications, it is essential to get everyone focused on the same goals. One must realize the more diverse the setting, the more important the communication. Clear, concise and timely communication helps to avoid many of the common concerns of a diverse school, district, organization and community.

Communications

- All written communication should be shared in English and in the language of the next largest minority or majority group.

- Written communication must be clear, jargon free, concise, positive and invitational.

- Whenever possible, follow up written communication with a phone call, meeting, or visit. A telephone alert system or calling system is very valuable for an urban school district.

- Start the school year with an all-student meeting to review expectations, rules and guidelines. All-school meetings and assemblies are effective ways to build a sense of family, spirit and unity in a diverse urban school setting.

- Get teachers to call parents with "good" news about a student at least one or two times per school year.

- School family nights for math, language arts, science, music concerts, and athletic events build unity and ownership in the school.

- Urban schools with Title I dollars could employ parent liaisons to bridge the communication gaps between the school and the homes.

- Parent education classes and support clinics can empower parents to help their children with school work.

- If any unusual event or bad event occurs in the school during the school day, parents should be notified by the end of the day with the information and how the school is dealing with the matter. Always try to avoid surprises for parents. If you don't tell them, the news media will.

- Many community people expect bad things to occur in urban schools. Therefore, it is essential to get parents, patrons and others to visit the schools. Visual communication is more powerful than oral communication or written communication.

The Orientation: Transition to the New School

In the urban setting, transitions and orientations are very important. Many parents or guardians have not experienced the greatest amount of success in urban schools and some are hesitant and apprehensive about the experience for their child. Other parents or guardians have had very positive experiences during their years in school, but they see story after story of negative things about public schools. As a result, they are apprehensive and reluctant about their child entering school. This same apprehension and doubt is present at each level of schooling. It starts with kindergarten and then continues in the move from kindergarten to first grade. This is followed by the big move from elementary school to middle school and then the huge jump from middle school to high school. In the urban setting, this school-level to school-level transition is further complicated by the increased mobility of many of the parents and children. The schools and the district can help decrease a great deal of the transition stress and anxiety by conducting transitional orientation programs and activities.

To Kindergarten With Love

The first time experiences are always unique. There is something about the fear of the unknown or the anxiety of the "new" happening. Many urban working parents have trusted their children to day care centers and Head Start programs before the children qualify for kindergarten. However, that doesn't reduce the excitement and apprehension of starting elementary school. The first task of the urban school district and the elementary school is to effectively communicate the kindergarten information to the community. Many schools have kindergarten round-ups. They work with day care centers, head start programs, churches, community centers, neighborhood associations, local media (television, radio, newspapers, and websites) and other organizations and people to seek out all young children who are eligible to attend kindergarten.

First Contact

- The rule of communication is simple. Keep the communication positive, informative and jargon free. Talk and write clearly and never attempt to impress anyone with your college words or education-speak language. Eliminate abbreviations from all communications.

- Provide assistance when needed and make the meeting places for registration as close to the parents as possible. If you have a high number of Hispanic/Latino parents and children, make sure that you work directly with the support agencies, centers and organizations. This is true of any minority group with high populations. Communicate written information in English and whatever the language of the largest minority student group. Have interpreters present to help communicate the information to parents.

Second Contact

- Once the students are registered for the kindergarten program, a letter and/or verbal follow-up message should be provided. This message should communicate how happy the school is to have their child as a new student. The message should be very positive and short.

- The next communicated message should be an invitation for the family and child to attend an open house or ice cream social or picnic to welcome everyone to the school. This is a key step in building a relationship. It is so important that the district should provide transportation to get the families to school if they do not have transportation. Providing transportation on the school bus the child will ride every day helps to break down another area of apprehension or concern. All of the teachers at the kindergarten level should be at the school's back-to-school social and families should be able to meet their child's principal, teacher, bus driver, cafeteria manager and custodian. If the school has parent liaisons, they should be a part of this "first" time school experience.

Third Contact

- The third contact is the first day of school. It should be a big deal. School personnel, the principal, kindergarten teachers and others should meet the new students as they depart from buses or cars. They should greet and welcome them and show them to their classes. Parents, who are available, should be invited for a special reception with coffee, juice, rolls, fruit, etc. They should be given a special greeting and be encouraged to stop by the school from time to time. There should be a brief review of how to get concerns addressed and a commitment to do the best possible job in educating their children.

This is a general outline for the welcome and orientation for an entering kindergarten child, but it should be repeated for all students new to an urban school at the start of a new school year.

From the Start to the Middle

There is no orientation and transition more valuable than the one from elementary school to middle school. It doesn't matter if the transition is from fifth grade to sixth grade or from sixth grade to seventh grade. The big deal is the change in schools or location; from a smaller elementary school to a large middle school; from working with one or two teachers to working with five to seven teachers. Add to these facility changes the physical changes that are starting to take place in the bodies and minds of the young students. Quite often the girls are getting taller and the boys are at various stages of growth. It is essential to get these children focused and excited about the next step in the education journey.

Orientation

First Contact

Middle school counselors visit elementary schools and communicate with the students about the middle school courses, activities and opportunities.

Second Contact

Elementary students visit middle schools and spend at least half of a day touring and meeting faculty.

Third Contact

Elementary parents and students are invited to an Information Night at the middle school. Questions about courses, curricula, music programs, athletic programs, schedules, clubs and activities are answered.

Transition Orientation

Before the start of the school year, a few days are scheduled for smaller groups of incoming elementary students to come to the middle school and spend a day of orientation, activities and traditions.

- The orientation team should be made up of eighth grade student leaders who have been trained to conduct the orientation activities. Teachers, parents and other school personnel are also allowed in the orientation. At the end of the activity day, all incoming students should know how to get around the school; how to get to the buses at the end of school; how to get to gym, the music room and all classroom areas; how to open lockers, if they have them; they should have their student ID pictures, if they need them; they should know the school colors, songs, special days and traditions; they should know about student dress requirements; and have a sense of what they will be expected to do to be successful in their new middle school.

- Transportation will be provided for the student orientations if needed.

- Lunch has to be provided so students understand the daily routine.

- If the school expects the students to keep up with their work, three-ringed binders or notebooks are recommended. Local merchants and vendors could help with some of these expenses.

The objective of the Transition Orientation is to get the students thinking about the new school, to get them excited about the possibilities; and to get them started in a positive manner. It should be informative and invitational.

From the Middle to the Top

The move from middle school to high school should be exciting. However, for so many urban students it looms as just another "thing" between them and getting away from their present circumstances. Too many are not properly prepared for the rigors of high school. But there is always the chance of changing those who don't want to come or those who know that they are not ready for the challenge. It is very important to get eighth graders to want to come to ninth grade at high school. In some cities, it might be ninth graders coming to tenth grade, but the challenge is the same. How do we keep them connected long enough to find a way to help them? One answer is a solid Transition/Orientation Program.

Transition Orientation

First Contact

High school counselors will visit middle schools and share curricula information about high school. Sometimes they might have high school performance arts groups to perform for the middle school students, e.g., jazz band, dancers, show choirs, singers, etc. Be sure that activities for all the students are presented. Other activities might be vocational programs, athletic opportunities as well as the arts.

Second Contact

Middle school students will visit high schools for a day or morning to receive information and tour the school.

Third Contact

An Information Night meeting for the parents of all middle school eighth graders should be held. This meeting will attempt to answer questions about high school credits for graduation, courses provided, activities, clubs, etc. The meeting will be held at the high school.

The Transition Orientation

- Incoming middle school students will be divided in alphabetical order and organized into different days for pre-school orientations. Some schools make it optional to attend; others require attendance, but it is still done before the start of the school year on the students' time.

- Upper-class juniors, seniors and unique sophomore student leaders are selected to join some faculty and staff members in conducting the orientation. Best results occur when the student leaders and faculty/staff leaders are provided leadership training before they work with the incoming freshmen.

- The orientation consists of a full day of activities connected with class identity, e.g., the class of 2010!; school traditions, e.g. school song, traditions; tours and orientation to the school; I.D. pictures; locker distributions, etc.

These activities get the new high school students feeling a part of the school and it breaks down many of those first school day anxieties and pressures.

Fourth Contact

For eighth grade students who may need additional help, there should be a special orientation with them and their parents to review all the resources available to help them be successful. They should be scheduled for a common daily class to get help with problems, homework or other concerns. There has to be a concerted effort to identify and help students who have been identified as being at-risk for and for dropping out of school. Even here, a different message can be communicated by the label applied to these students. Instead of referring to them as "at-risk" perhaps they can be referred to as "at-opportunity" students.

Media Relations

Student orientations and communications are the backbone of an urban school's success. The media outlets must know what is happening in the schools and they need to know as much of the "why" as possible. These simple dimensions take a giant leap when the media communicates information about schools in urban settings.

- Opening School Student Meetings

Once school is in session, there should be opening school meetings for students. These meetings are important in elementary schools, but in urban middle schools and high schools they are very important. These meetings can be by classes, e.g. first, second, and third grades together or individually. At middle school they could be grouped by sixth or seventh grade boys or girls, or all sixth and seventh grade students. The rule is what accommodates the comfort level and effectiveness of the presenter or the information presented. These are really not the normal student assemblies. These meetings are focused on direct, clear and informative communication. It should center on expectations, observations, history, school traditions or practices. They touch upon citizenship, respect and purpose. The following points could make these meetings more relevant and engaging:

- Keep the meetings to thirty minutes or less.

- Have teachers cover some routine information in the days before the meeting.

- Provide some visual information.

- Try to incorporate music in some way.

- Don't allow the meeting to be just talking heads.

- Create some follow-up activity or contest to get the students thinking and talking.

- Administrators help teachers by having such meetings in the afternoons and they help themselves by having them early in the morning.

- Where possible, include data. This is especially true of using their data or other data they can relate to easily.

- Make sure it's a talk "up" meeting and not a talk "down" meeting.

- Try very hard to convey the fact that you care about every one of them and you want to help them succeed.

When used properly, the opening school student meetings can be a valuable means to unite students around some common "norms," "expectations" and "hopes."

- Connect the School to Home with a Phone Message System

In the frantic world of urban education and schooling, many things occur during the school day. Most of them are planned, but too many just happen.

A student might bring a gun to school and create more suspense and activities than an administrator cares to handle. However, it must be handled and it must be done the "right" way. There is no doubt that one gun will result in hundreds of stories and tales. Many might be true, but a few will be totally off mark. Sending a letter home with each elementary student might work, but the letters won't be as reliable when we entrust them to middle school and high school students.

Now there is a great way to utilize a telephone calling system that allows the principal to share the story with the parents, even before the child gets home. These calling systems are invaluable in emergency situations, but they are also wonderful for communicating other important information to parents, e.g. reminder about meetings, special school programs, notice of report cards coming home, school news, etc. The message on the system can be given in English, Spanish and other languages. This is a simple way to create and maintain great communication between the school and the home. For parents without phones, a special call-in number could be provided for updates and information. In case of emergency local media could direct parents to contact a special information number for emergency news and updates.

One of the grand ironies is that with all the technology and multiple means of communication, we have more parents uninformed than there were in the latter years of the 20th Century. Potential for communication means very little until we take it upon ourselves to communicate! In the urban school setting, multiple means and efforts must be employed to establish, maintain and continue communication between the school and the home. It is just too easy to make an excuse because of deprivations, poverty and other common realities. One of the fundamental hopes for success in urban schools is personal contacts and communication.

Media Suggestions

In too many urban school situations media relations is often about the latest bad news story. These stories range from district test scores, financial problems, poor test scores, weapons in school, poor student choices, parent or other complaints, superintendent dismissals, teacher shortages, conflicts with other governmental units, union problems or concerns, high dropout rates, low graduation rates, etc. Urban school districts can fall back and receive one media hit after another one, or districts can decide to take a proactive approach. There is so much good news, so many positive achievements, acts, etc., that never make the news. Districts have to establish some media and/or communication outlets to tell the other stories to the public. The following media suggestions are not new, but they really can help urban school districts counter some of the negative impact of media.

School Community Relations

Urban districts frequently have no funding for positions to tell the schools' stories to the media and community. But it is too important to communicate the message to wait until there is money. Positive communication often can result in attracting money. The urban school district needs a community relations person to work with media and others to tell the school's story. Parent volunteers and others could help out in this area, but a qualified person is essential to get the job done.

The media relations or community relations position is essential in changing the negative perception of the urban school district. This individual will work with the superintendent, school principals, central office administrators, police officers, radio and television outlets, newspapers and other print media to effectively communicate the message. The message might be negative or positive, but this person will effectively get it out in the most professional manner possible.

The media/community relations person should become the first or second voice for the district. Often the superintendent is the first voice. However, this media relations person should help clarify the voice of the superintendent. It is possible to have the superintendent to directly communicate only positive news and the media relations person can communicate the other news. This has a stronger positive result for the superintendent than most people would think.

The media relations person builds a bridge from the school district to the community. This person seeks and establishes community contacts, works with parents and others to support school district initiatives and creates media contact persons at each school and district facility.

The Press: Editorial Board Meeting

The urban school superintendent should have a working relationship with all media outlets. However, it is essential to have an open communication with the largest daily newspaper. It is this paper that often will assign a reporter to cover district news, school board meetings, and special events. A superintendent or school leader may not always agree with news stories, but it is key to keep open communication with the community's largest newspaper. One effective strategy is to schedule at least one editorial meeting with the newspaper editors each school year. There are some key points to remember in participating in an editorial board meeting:

- Everything is on the record! Don't say or share anything that you don't want the community to know.

- Plan ahead for the meeting. It is not an opportunity to throw around ideas and possibilities

- Communicate your plans, concerns, strategies, etc., in clear, concise language

- Share important upcoming programs and activities

- Never go to an editorial board with a plan to attack them for something printed or reported prior to the meeting. You may need clarification or have questions about a story or report, but it should not be an attack. "Never pick a fight with anyone who buys ink by the gallon."

Remember, newspapers in urban areas are impacted by many of the same urban forces that impact urban school districts. When possible, communicate from this shared urban point of view. Seek ways to expand positive ways for the newspaper to cover school activities and programs.

Media: The Message and Urban Setting

There are many negatives created by operating in urban school districts. Issues such as crime, health care, housing, homelessness, transportation, taxes, etc., are constantly impacting urban schools and the families and children in them. However, the urban setting also provides many opportunities to get the word out about school programs and activities.

Themes and Campaigns

Urban schools can get a great deal of exposure and support for district or school campaigns. All the media and news outlets are eager to report a "new" something or a unique activity. We have enjoyed success with the Back-to-School theme campaign. Recently our campaign to have fathers bring their children to school on the first day really created tremendous attention and support. We utilize the neighborhood weeklies, the main newspaper, billboards and the television and radio media. We did not place placards on city buses, nor did we circulate community flyers, but we were very successful in getting the word out.

The urban setting brings people to similar places, activities and events. These places, activities and events create great opportunities to communicate the school's message. People get their hair cut or prepared a few times per month. Most of the time that they are in the barber shop or the beauty shop they are waiting. When they wait, they will talk and they will read. It becomes very important to get school information into these shops. This also applies to churches, grocery stores, shopping centers and other outlets. Most neighborhoods have councils or associations and they meet a few times per year. It is important to get information out to them. The city government has the name of community associations and organizations that can help communicate the school's message.

The urban city is a network of neighborhoods, communities and organizations. The effective school district media program is connected to all of these opportunities to spread the message.

Chapter 1 Case Studies

Case Study 1: Suburban

You are the superintendent in a suburban school district in a town of approximately 15,000 people and your school district (3,200 students) has seen an increase in the student Hispanic population climb from 12 percent to 32 percent over a seven-year period. Local community members have called for a communitywide forum and asked you to be on a panel to discuss the "immigrant problem." In advance, you are given the following questions to be prepared to address in the forum. Discuss how you would respond. In addition, what kind of data would you need in supporting your responses?

- Why is it that we are spending our tax dollars to educate non-citizens in our schools?

- Would we be able to meet state and federal student achievement levels if the Hispanic population was not a part of our school system?

- Does the fact that one third of the students in our district are Hispanic slow down or hinder the educational opportunities for children of non-Hispanic families?

- What are you able to do to stop the entrance of illegal students into our schools?

Case Study 2: Urban

You are a superintendent of a mid-size (50,000 students) urban school district. Due to a tremendous drop in your student enrollment, you have been forced to close four middle schools. Two of the middle schools will have to be combined with a third middle school, creating the largest middle school in the school district. The two middle schools being combined with the third middle school are both very different. One of the middle schools is 60 percent African American, 20 percent White, 15 percent Hispanic/Latino and 5 percent "other." It failed to meet Adequate Yearly Progress (AYP) and was reconstructed three years ago, and now it is the most improved middle school in the district. It has the highest percentage of special education students among the district's middle schools, above 30 percent. The other middle school is more than 50 percent Hispanic/Latino, 20 percent African American, 30 percent White, and it has failed to reach AYP for the last three years.

Based upon your understanding of this chapter, create a plan to effectively:

- Communicate the information to parents and the community.
- Create an Orientation and Transition plan for this change.
- Create an opening of school media plan for the middle school.

Case Study 3: Rural

A rural school with a population of less than 500 has to prepare for a pending drop in revenue collections because of an enrollment decline. The decrease in revenue must be addressed by decreasing expenditure; a reduction in personnel expenditures appears to be the most effective method. Four teachers have expressed their plans to retire, but would like to continue as part-time classroom teachers. All four teachers have twenty years of experience but each of the four has been ineffective multiculturally. However, all four are reading specialists and the district is a mandated reading improvement plan, and two of them are needed as part-time teachers. Based on the knowledge that you have gained from this chapter, develop a list of questions to ask each teacher; the response of each teacher will be used as part of the decision of who you will ask to return.

Chapter 2

Effective Instructional Supervision

Rural Perspective

Equality is the heart and essence of democracy, freedom and justice.

—Phillip Randolph

Teaching multiculturally requires that one consider all factors that make students unique. This diversity must be diversity throughout, and incorporated into the learning process. To assess this practice the administrator must first envision it; you must know it in order to recognize it.

Teaching multiculturally requires one to consider all factors that make students different yet unique, and incorporate these factors into the instructional process. Race, ethnicity, gender, and social class must be woven into the fabric of the curriculum (the course). There is no recipe that works for all students, but to assess and experience effective instructional supervision, the administrator must know it when he sees it.

The following is a list of objectives that an administrator may consider as he/she evaluates and supervises the instructional effectiveness within the classroom. While the classroom teacher bears the fundamental responsibility to provide instruction, the site administrator must serve as the instructional leader. The site administrator should look for and assess the level to which the classroom teacher performs in the following areas:

- Teacher Management Indicators
    - o   Preparation – The teacher plans for the delivery of lessons relative to short-term and long-term objectives.
    - o   Routine – The teacher uses minimum class time for non-instructional routines.

- o Discipline – The teacher clearly defines expected behavior (encourages positive behavior and controls negative behavior).

- o Learning Environment – The teacher establishes rapport with students and provides a pleasant, safe, and orderly environment conducive to learning.

- Teacher Instructional Indicators

  - o Establishes Objectives – The teacher communicates the instructional objective to students.

  - o Stresses Sequence – The teacher shows how the present topic relates to those previously taught or that will be taught.

  - o Relates Objectives – The teacher relates the subject topic to existing student experiences.

  - o Involves All Learners – The teacher uses signaled responses, questioning techniques and guided practices to involve all learners.

  - o Explains Content – The teacher uses a variety of methods to explain the lesson.

  - o Explains Directions – The teacher gives clearly stated directions that are related to the learning objective.

  - o Models – The teacher demonstrates the desired skills.

  - o Monitors – The teacher checks to determine how each student is progressing toward the stated objective.

o Adjusts Based On Monitoring – The teacher changes instruction based on the results of monitoring.

o Guides the Practice – The teacher requires all students to practice the newly acquired skills while under the direct supervision of the teacher.

o Provides for Independent Practice – The teacher requires all students to practice the newly acquired skills without direct supervision.

o Established Closure – The teacher summarizes and fits into context what has been taught.

- Teacher Product Indicator

  o Lesson Plans – The teacher writes daily lesson plans designed to achieve the identified objectives.

  o Student Files – The teacher maintains a written record of student progress.

  o Grading Patterns – The teacher maintains a grading pattern that is based on identified criteria and administered fairly.

- Student Achievement Indicators – Students demonstrate mastery of the stated objectives through projects, daily assignments, performance and test scores (Minimum Criteria for Effective Teacher, Oklahoma State Department of Education).

Suburban Perspective

The quality of the education system cannot exceed the quality of its teachers.

—Barber & Mourshed, 2007

Who Do We Select?

This seemingly obvious statement should be the central focus for any administrator when it comes to ensuring that instructional supervision is effective and successful. This principle is also fully applicable regardless of the educational setting, socio-economic status, student makeup, or size of a school system. In short, great teachers can become good supervisors of learning and will end up making any school community meet its intended goals for learning.

The administrator who wants to meet such intended goals needs to seek out those "great" teachers and create conditions that allow them to take the lead in becoming the trend setters for the rest of the teaching staff. In a diverse school setting, there are many qualities exhibited by those great teachers. Three in particular are critical to success in a diverse setting. They are a dedication to equity in learning opportunities for their students, a commitment to pursue excellence (both for their students and for themselves), and finally, a desire to be the trend setters in teaching for their buildings.

If the administrator in a diverse student population school setting can hire, encourage, and support such teachers, successful instructional supervision will happen in that school. It may not occur overnight, but with time and the right amount of administrative support, there will be significant change in the process of teachers leading and improving the instructional process in the classroom. The good administrator finds these people and supports them without getting in their way.

The effective school district leader is aware that finding the right people to meet the needs of the diverse population they serve is not a task that can be taken lightly. A systematic approach in screening, interviewing and selecting these staff members is essential. Each district may be different in the process they use, but the more diverse the educational setting, the more important it is to be sure staff members and potential staff members understand the diverse makeup of the school community and that members of the community feel they are represented, or at least heard, as to the needs of their children.

Time and effort should be expended in crafting the initial and subsequent interviews to be sure the candidates—whether teachers, support staff or school leaders—understand the needs of the students of the district and are a good match for the existing staff and the school corporation itself.

Once the candidate has been selected as a part of the team, providing pre-service orientation and education is essential to making sure the new staff member is integrated into the culture and climate of the school and understands what their role is in meeting the needs of the students and community.

The Administrator's Challenge

Hopefully, the reader has inferred by now that the term "instructional supervision" does not fall only on the administrator and his powers of good supervision. It truly is an impossible task to achieve if a principal or superintendent thinks he or she can become the sole person responsible for leading the things that occur in the classroom. I will re-emphasize, it is the teacher who really becomes the supervisor of instruction and the administrator is really the facilitator of that process.

The next logical question though for the administrator is how he or she can make the conditions and the environment right for this process to take place. It starts by the administrator knowing the internal makeup of his or her teachers. The administrator needs to have a framework of assessing the teacher so they can know what he or she must do to enhance the weak areas and utilize the strengths of the teacher so that they become that great teacher you desire. Mary M. Kennedy has suggested that a framework for us would be to divide teacher qualities into three groups. These are their personal resources, their performance qualities, and their effectiveness (Kennedy, 2008). Personal resources would include personality traits, knowledge, and skills of content, and their teaching credentials (degrees and training). Performance qualities include their ability to interact with others, classroom organizational skills, types of instruction they use in the classroom (higher order thinking). The effectiveness quality refers to how well they support student learning (test scores), how they motivate students, and how they lead both in and outside the school. A good administrator can quickly use these three categories to effectively assess whether or not a teacher has the ability to be a good instructional supervisor and thus impact the climate for learning in a building.

The wise administrator hopes that great teachers use their skills to influence other teachers, thus impacting instruction in the district. For this to occur, the district leader must show by action and belief that they want teachers to be empowered to improve in all three areas. We have all seen teachers who may have one or two of the areas but severely lack in the other. A teacher may have great knowledge base of subject matter, but not have the skill set to impart the knowledge to the students of his/her diverse classroom. As district leader, you must convince your Board and community that it is imperative to continue to enhance all your staff's ability to serve at the highest level. To do this you must assess the needs of all your staff—both certificated and support staff—and provide professional development opportunities to meet their identified needs.

A mistake made frequently is that district leaders decide what the needs of their staff are and do not ask for input from the very stakeholders they are trying to serve. To develop this sense of community and shared needs assessment, the leader should not decide in a vacuum what the staff needs to be better able to perform their duties. By establishing an open forum for input as to professional development needs and also by using available data on student and district performance, a more specific plan for staff improvement can be designed.

At the conclusion of any program or identified area of emphasis, an assessment should be completed to see if the program actually made a difference and whether the needs of the staff were met so they can do a more effective job of meeting the needs of the student population.

Further Facilitation

Many times school corporations believe that only outside "experts" can facilitate the improvement and/or change they have identified to assist staff members. Many times we fail to realize we have highly qualified staff members in our organizations who can champion change and improved instruction. Most of our great teachers can lead the charge to improvement, and this can have benefits for more than just improved instruction. The sense of ownership and improved morale can be sidebar benefits from using our own staff to lead improvement efforts.

After the administrator has identified the teacher they want to lead the process of improvement, the next step is to create a positive environment in which they can thrive. The single most important factor to make this environment positive for them in the diverse student population district is to create time for them to interact with other teachers in a dialogue about classroom instruction. With this being said, it is also one of the most difficult things to accomplish for an administrator. In most public school districts, designated professional development time outside of the 180 instructional days is usually measured in a few hours instead of days. Creativity and a dedication to finding extra time during the regular instructional day is requisite if you truly want to provide those great teachers with that needed time for instructional dialogue. When that opportunity is provided to the teacher, the natural result is a professional learning community in which the sharing of knowledge is valued. Michael Fullan defines that outcome very succinctly. "If you want to develop leadership, you should focus on reciprocity the mutual obligation and value of sharing knowledge among organizational members" (Fullan, 2001). It is our responsibility as educational leaders to make sure sharing of knowledge takes place regularly among our teaching leaders.

Levels of Instruction and Supervision

Although not one of the most pleasant parts of the position of either principal or superintendent, the idea of assessing and evaluating performance is an integral part of the position of leadership. Many leaders will use the excuse of lack of time to explain away why the process of evaluation is not completed effectively. There is NO excuse for not doing effective formative and summative evaluations on all staff. Normally the superintendent or designee will assess building leaders, and building leaders will assess their respective staffs. For too many years this has been accomplished with some simplistic Lickert scale or completed in a haphazard manner, and when completed all that can be said is something has been done, but no emphasis on continuous improvement or meeting the needs of a diverse population has been addressed.

In recent years many school corporations have taken an active lead in changing the paradigm of what evaluation has been in the past and looked for new ways to assess staff and identify ways to improve instruction. Many have begun to develop rubrics with input from all stakeholders to show what effective teaching and leading is and how those being assessed can demonstrate mastery of specific identified measures of effectiveness. Once areas of need are identified, it is then the leader's responsibility and opportunity to develop specific professional development opportunities for all staff to improve.

In many districts in the suburban setting, there is a lack of diversity when it comes to ethnicity. This is not a reason for a void in this type of professional development activities. In some districts, including the one I serve, there is a great deal of diversity and, as has been stated before, our Hispanic population has grown much faster than our staff turnover has taken place. So to keep our existing staff members effective in meeting the changing diverse population, specific professional development activities must be designed so that existing and new staff members can be educated, and allowed to put into practice what they learn so they can have an understanding of the students they serve. In those suburban districts that have little ethnic diversity, it is still imperative the staff understand diversity so they can address it and prepare their students for the world in which they will be living and not in the micro -culture they live in as they attend school.

Urban Perspective

This view of instructional supervision totally belongs to this author! I will cite one reference and will not quote anyone else. This is purely my view ascertained from years of work and observations. I make no apologies and I am seeking no agreement from others. However, I have held these views for too long and I am relieved to share them.

Teachers and Instruction

In the urban setting or in any educational setting, no one is as important to instruction and to its supervision as the classroom teacher. The teacher is the essential factor in the quality and effectiveness of the instruction provided to students. The teacher determines how the instruction is imparted; in what proportions or quantities; and the feedback, remediation and enrichment provided. There is no one more valuable to instruction and to learning than the teacher.

The quality of a teacher's instruction is determined by the subject knowledge, general knowledge and life experiences of the teacher. The ability to impart or to share that knowledge is determined by presentation skills, practices, creativity, innovation, and common sense. In spite of the knowledge accumulated by a teacher in a subject, the teacher has to understand the needs and deprivation of the student with no clue or understanding of the subject. The teacher has to relate to the students and their various levels of blankness in order to effectively teach them what they need to know. It is truly impossible to "teach what you don't know."

In urban schools, teachers must know their subject matter and be able to teach it in multiple ways to multiple learners. This flexibility of instruction is needed to make instruction relevant to various students with diverse learning styles.

However, one of the great problems in urban education is teachers providing instruction in subjects in which they are not certified and often not qualified to teach. This is especially true in the areas of Mathematics, Science and Special Education. It violates the first rule of teaching: "You can't teach what you don't know."This practice compromises the education of too many children in urban schools. Districts and states attempt to overcome these "out of subjects" teaching problems with emergency licenses, special college courses, and various staff development strategies. Instruction is just too important to be presented poorly or inappropriately.

It is common to hear about teachers teaching subjects for which they are not certified in urban schools. However, it is just as common to find the veteran or most experienced teaching the best students. This often results in the new teachers, who are often first or second year teachers, teaching the most difficult students. This creates tremendous problems for the students with the most difficulties in learning and in controlling their behavior. Young teachers, with little or no teaching experience, assigned to teach the most difficult students are simply a formula for failure. A few, but very few, teachers survive and get another year to try to move up to better students, but too many of these young teachers are compromised by the experience. Teachers want to teach! Too often in these low level classes teaching is an afterthought. This brings us to that term of "supervision."Who is responsible for the supervision of instruction? We know that the teacher has the primary responsibility for knowing the subject and imparting that knowledge. But who makes sure that teachers do their jobs and who is responsible to make sure that classroom conditions, supplies and supports are in place to ensure that teachers can do their jobs?

Administrators and Instructional Supervision

It is so simple to place all of the duty on the school principal. The school principal is responsible for the supervision of instruction. But this is too simple to be totally true. Yes, the principal is the point person and he/she will take the victory or defeat. However, the responsibility for instruction starts at the top of the district. School boards make policy that mandate instruction for all students. Boards are responsible for policy and they are responsible for employing a superintendent to carry out the policy. The superintendent must follow the mandates of the board's policy. To do that, the superintendents, in the urban districts, employ assistant superintendents and/or directors to implement board policy. These assistants and/or directors employ coordinators, supervisors and school principals to enforce or carry out the board policy. The principal and assistant are the last administrative contact before the act of instruction is carried out. They touch the teacher and the teacher instructs the students. Support for the teacher and instruction must come from the principal; supervision of instruction must come from the principal. However, support for the principal and teacher should come from the Board, the superintendents and all the support levels between the top and the school. This is the ideal alignment of responsibility and duty. However, in too many places this alignment does not exist when blame is involved. The No Child Left Behind Law tried to connect a school's Adequate Yearly Progress (AYP) to a District's Adequate Yearly Progress, but the restructuring and major impact is still on the school principal and the faculty of the school.

Principals and Instructional Supervision

The "buck stops" with the school principal in supervision of instruction. The principal has to observe, evaluate, support, terminate and pro-vide staff development activities to help improve the achievement of all students. These duties can be viewed in the following manner:

- Observe – The term supervision really means "super"-"vision."The principal has to be out and about. I tell principals to do "People by day and paper by night."It means don't be in your office doing paperwork when children and teachers are in the building. Get out there and "see" what is happening.

  - Create short five- to ten-minute classroom walk-throughs. Create a checklist of things to look for in each walk-through. Informally give feedback to teachers of what you observed. These points may be good or bad, but they are just feedback for improvement.

  - Do school walk-arounds with the custodian once a week to observe the building and its needs.

  - Walk the school playground frequently to check for safety concerns. In high schools, check the campus at least once per month for concerns.

- Evaluate – The most important duty of a school principal is evalu-ation of teacher instruction. A principal must know and be able to communicate the parts of "effective" teaching. This is more important than "good" teaching. Effective teaching is measured by the performance of the students. What are the results of their work; what are they able to demonstrate? "Good" teaching is often centered on what the teacher is doing, but the "good" becomes the "ugly" if the students can't demonstrate positive results from the "good" teaching. It is the principal's duty to ensure effective instruction for students.

- Terminate – Teacher unions often receive the blame for poor teachers in the teaching profession. However, in this matter the unions have received a bad rap. School principals are the primary cause of most of the poor teachers in the teaching profession. If the first year teacher is not ready to teach, why do we allow the teacher to come back for the second year? Too many principals have bet on improvement without putting in the improvement plan and the work that goes with making the plan effective. You can't "hope" a poor teacher into a good teacher. I still haven't seen a union contract that prevents principals from terminating a poor first year teacher. Unions can be blamed for how some teachers dress, but they shouldn't be blamed for how they teach. That responsibility resides with the principal.

- Support – In fairness to first year teachers, especially those placed with the toughest students, there should be a support system. It starts with a principal who does everything possible to make the classroom climate and conditions acceptable for teaching. It includes some of the following supports:

  - Discipline – Make sure students and parents know that no student will be allowed to destroy the educational chances of others in the classroom.

  - Students have a time-out or in-school suspension alternative when they disrupt the classroom.

  - Support the teacher in communicating learning expectations with parents.

  - Urban districts have to create alternative programs and/or schools for students who are not successful in the regular school setting.

- Ensure that new teachers are not always assigned to the toughest students; schedule veteran teachers to help with some of the most challenging students.

- Staff Development – Effective supervision of instruction can not occur without the means to improve the skills and expertise of teachers and administrators. The following areas of staff development are frequently needed in urban settings:

   - Effective communications

   - Invitational practices

   - Subject area instruction for Mathematics, Language Arts/ English, Science, Social Studies, Music, Art and Physical Education

   - Writing

   - Reading

   - Discipline

   - Curriculum mapping

   - Date driven instruction

   - Improving instruction via data review

   - Technology: Hardware, software, others

   - Special education

   - English language learners

   - Title I assortment of activities and trainings

These and other topics are frequently covered in order to improve schools instructional programs and practices. Almost every one of them is related to improving instruction for students. School principals must keep the focus on improving instruction for students.

Levels of Instruction and Supervision

There are many additional facets of instructional supervision and they all impact the quality of the education urban students receive. However, I could not end this look at instructional supervision without sharing a concern on the levels of instruction in urban schools. Many researchers and educators have indicated that suburban senior students, on average, graduate with a twelvth grade education and urban senior students, on average, graduate with an eighth grade education. This, on average, has proven to be truer than I care to admit. The question is, why?

The primary reason, based upon my observation and research, is found in the literacy level of the urban teachers and urban students. Literacy opens the doors to understanding and creates the construction of mental bridges to higher enlightenment and thoughts. True literacy creates thoughts, questions and sometimes answers. The level of literacy obtained by students truly separates them and how they react to their societies. According to Patrick J. Finn in his outstanding book, *Literacy with an Attitude*, there are four levels of literacy:

- The "performance level" is the lowest. It simply is the ability to sound out words and turn sentences that are common in informal face-to-face conversation into writing. Most fourth and fifth graders are competent at this level.

- The "functional level" is the ability to read and write to meet the demands of an average day of an average person, such as reading USA Today, filling out a job application, understanding directions for using simple machines, or writing a note to another person. Children learn functional literacy. They simply follow the directions given to them.

- The "informational level" of literacy is the ability to read and absorb the kind of knowledge needed to write examinations and reports based on what was read. The informational knowledge is normally associated with getting the information right. However, it rarely involves creativity.

- The "powerful literacy level" involves creativity and reason. It is the kind of literacy that breeds critical thinking, the ability to evaluate, to analyze and to synthesize. It is one thing to be able to read the words of others, but it is more powerful to be able to create your own thoughts and words. (Finn, 2000)

If we examine Patrick J. Finn's four levels of literacy and compare them with Benjamin Bloom's Taxonomy levels of instruction, we can answer most of the "why" question in the gap between the performance of suburban high school senior graduates and urban high school senior graduates. The "performance level of literacy" is aligned with Bloom's knowledge and comprehension levels. Finn's "functional level" is aligned with Bloom's comprehension, application levels. Finn's "informational level" is aligned with Bloom's comprehension, application and analysis levels. Finally, Finn's "powerful literacy level" is aligned with Bloom's analysis, synthesis, and evaluation levels.

Teachers in urban settings frequently do a good job of imparting instruction at the knowledge, comprehension and application levels of learning. This is equal to the functional level of literacy. It often involves just giving back information shared, researched or taught. This is competence at the seventh grade level. Taking this to a level of instructing through knowledge, comprehension, application and analysis is at the eighth to lower ninth grade level. This brings a student to the lower level of the "informational level of literacy."This is often the highest point for many urban school students. This level of learning will allow students to graduate, go to college and get mid to high level manager jobs. If the students have acquired technical skills, this level will allow the student to be successful at the management, repair and support levels.

However, many of the students in top suburban high schools, prep schools and some private schools are instructed at the next highest level of powerful literacy. They are taught to think and be creative through analysis, synthesis and evaluation. They are instructed to question the answer, not to just accept it. They are instructed to seek out, research, and create new knowledge, new thoughts and new ideas.

The essential difference in the levels of literacy and the levels of instruction is the expertise, skills and talents of the teacher. Sure, many of these suburban prep and private schools will have numerous supplies, resources and revenue to support experiences, applications, enrichment and more. But the fundamental difference maker is in the quality of the teachers. The teacher is certified and teaching in an area of expertise, or maybe not certified but blessed with more experiences than an education in a subject area can ever provide. The Adequate Yearly Progress (AYP) term of "highly qualified teacher" often is relegated to a meaning of meeting subject certification requirements. In this sense, one can be a dance teacher without ever being an outstanding dancer. As a matter of fact, one can be a dance teacher without knowing how to truly do more than one dance or maybe no dance at all. But to be a great teacher, one has to get students to know dance and movement, to know space and time, to feel and know the beat and rhythm. They will be able to know, comprehend apply, analyze, synthesize and evaluate the activity of dance. They will know how to create new dance, they will innovate, rearrange and evaluate. They will know dance.

The urban schools have some very talented students and they will rise and fall based upon the quality of the instruction imparted to them. Administrators must do everything possible to ensure that urban instruction is the very best that it can be. There is no safety net. Powerful literacy and powerful instruction will result in powerful urban students and better urban centers for our future.

Chapter 2 Case Studies

Case Study 1: Rural

While considering the concepts taught in this chapter, choose 3-5 of the indicators, listed as minimum criteria for effective teaching that reflect an emphasis on culture and identify at least one method that a classroom teacher can use to apply cultural considerations to the indicator.

Case Study 2: Suburban

You have had a large increase in your Hispanic population over the past seven years. You still have many staff members who were here before the increase and some still have not yet embraced the new "look" of your school system. You now have five openings for staff from elementary to secondary. How will you go about designing the interview process? What will the makeup of your interview committee be?

1. Write at least five questions to ask all candidates that will be legal while still going to the heart of what kind of candidate you need.

2. Design a professional development activity (just in types of activities to use) that will be able to meet needs of existing and new staff members for the first day of next school year.

Case Study 3: Urban

You are the superintendent of an urban system. You have a principal of an urban high school of 1,500 students. You have an English department of ten teachers. Four of the ten teachers are retiring at the end of this school year. Ironically, the four retiring English teachers all teach the best students in the school. For years, new teachers entering the high school have been assigned to teaching the lowest level of students with the toughest behavior problems. As the new superintendent you have mandated that the principal correct this teacher assignment problem in each department by using retirement to phase in the change. What process will you use to make the needed change in the English department?

Chapter 3

Political Implications

Rural Perspective

Leadership is influence, nothing more, nothing less.

—John Maxwell

One must never underestimate the political implications of leadership. The strengths and weaknesses of the school administrators are known and perceived by the members of the community. Regardless of the local, state, and national reports or the effectiveness of public schools, when one administrator analyzes the grass root effects of local leadership, he/she will discover that many of the decisions made recently are entangled in politics. According to Edgar Schein (1999), one of the most consistent findings by historians, sociologists, and social psychologists is that what leadership should be depends on the particular situation, the task to be performed, and the characteristics of the leader's subordinates; the culture of the organization will determine the type of leadership; type of leadership will have political implications.

Every organization has a culture, a pattern of basic assumptions that a given group has invented, discovered or developed while learning to cope with the problems of external adaptation and internal integration. Such culture is the driving force of the daily operation of the school or organization, and can be divided into three basic components (core values, mission, and vision). All three impact the daily operation of the school or organization because each is reflective of the leader. Core values are the basic assumptions of the school or organization and are a part of the organizational culture. These core values may entail living above reproach, developing character, and walking in integrity. They are prerequisite to the mission and vision of the organization. Mission is the process toward the vision. It is the star that guides the school or organization. The mission is simply a short yet compelling statement that addresses the needs, expectations and values of the group being served. The mission will underscore the leadership and integrity of the school or organization. It is through the mission that one can get a true picture of the organizational culture. Vision is the ultimate goal of the school or organization. Through vision, the reason for the existence of the school or organization and the cause or motive that leads to action is underscored. The passion of the leader, as expressed in the school organization, along with his/her motivational driving force are all part of the vision (Schein, 1999).

There is considerable diversity in leadership styles for schools or organizations. However, one type of leadership that impacts the political implications of leadership in a rural district is servant leadership, a model first developed by Robert Greenleaf. It emphasizes increased service to others, a holistic approach to work, promoting a sense of community and shared power in decision making. A servant leader is one who is a servant first. Servant leadership begins with a conscious choice of one who inspires to lead and to make sure the highest priorities of the people being served are met diligently (Greenleaf, 2003). The true test of servant leadership can be answered as one asks the following:

- Do those served grow as people?

- Do they, while being served, become healthier, wiser, freer, more autonomous, more likely themselves to become servants?

Servant leadership deals with the reality of power in everyday life; it deals with legitimacy, ethical restraints upon it, and the beneficial results that can be attained through the appropriate set of power. There are ten characteristics of a servant leader:

1. Listening – Identifying and clarifying the will of the group and

getting in touch with one's own choice to understand the personal body, spirit and the mind of communication.

2. Healing – Using the opportunity of service to help others become whole again after suffering from broken spirits and emotional stress.

3. Awareness – A general self-awareness that lends itself to being able to view situations from an integrated holistic approach.

4. Empathy – Understanding, recognizing, and accepting the special and unique character of others.

5. Persuasion – Leadership through convincing others rather than compliance.

6. Conceptualization – Looking at the school or organization and planning for the school or organization beyond the day-to-day realities.

7. Foresight – The ability to foresee a possible outcome or a situation; understanding the lessons from the past, the realities of the present, and the likely consequences of the decisions for the future.

8. Stewardship – Holding the school or organization in trust for the general good of the society.

9. Commitment to the growth of people – Recognizing the tremendous responsibility to do everything within reason to nurture the personal, professional, and spiritual growth of the followers.

10. Building community – Seeking to identify the means to replace the lost human history resulting from the shifts from local communities to large institutions (Greenleaf, 2003).

C. William Pollard uses servant leadership as the basic framework of organizational philosophy for his company, ServiceMaster. The philosophy used by Pollard has three goals:

- To honor and realize the potential of every employee
- To recognize the dignity and worth of every employee
- To commit the organization to developing and supporting each employee

This is enforced by the guiding principle to honor God, to help people develop, to pursue excellence, and to grow profitably. Pollard also lists several characteristics of a servant leader:

- Commitment to leadership
- Initiator of change
- Giver rather than taker
- Promoter of diversity
- Values driven
- Performance oriented

Continuing with servant leadership, from the religious perspective, C. G. Wilkes posits that servant leaders follow seven basic principles:

- Humble your heart – Recognize the difference between pride and the authentic confidence in the source; allow God to work in your life.
- Be a follower – A servant leader will follow Christ rather than seek a position.
- Find greatness in service – Give up personal rights and find greatness in service to others; move from self-interest to stewardship.

- Take risks – Be a pioneer rather than a settler; take a risk, go out and make the territory safe for others (settlers).

- Take up the towel – Lead from a kneeling position and take up Jesus' towel of servanthood to meet the needs of others. Nehemiah is a good example of such a servant leader. His concern, compassion and humility caused his heart to break and with such he moved from self-service to service for others.

- Share responsibility and authority – Share this to meet the greater need of others by encouraging them, understanding them, equipping them, qualifying them, instructing them, and praying for them.

- Build a team – Include the followers in what you do by creating a sense of togetherness, empowering with authority and presence, accounting for the mission and team success, being a mentor (Wilkes, 1998).

All of these authors (Greenleaf, Pollard, and Wilkes) share common values of leadership and they are expressed in the following ways:

- Leadership is influence—nothing more, nothing less. Leadership differs from management in that leadership is the ability to influence people to follow while management is maintaining systems and processes.

- Trust is the foundation for leadership. In order to build such trust, a leader must exemplify competence, connection, and character. A leader can not break trust and expect to continue to influence people; violate the trust and you're finished as the leader.

- People will naturally follow leaders who are stronger than themselves. Leaders think in terms of the direction they want to go (vision) and also who will follow them. The level of leadership within a person also allows the person to recognize leadership or the lack of it in other people.

- Successful leaders empower others. The capacity of people to achieve is determined by the ability of the leader to empower. Empowering others or training them to take over your job is the greatest way to prove invincibility. Empowering is powerful for the mentor and the person being developed because enlarging others makes you large.

- It takes a leader to raise another leader. The only way to do this is to become a better leader yourself and to remember that leaders see the big picture, attract potential leaders, offer incentives, encourage creativity, allow for risks and provide accountability.

- The lasting value of a leader is measured by succession. The leader must prepare the organization to live in the absence of the leader. A legacy is created when a leader puts the organization in a position to do great things without him. A leader's focus must be to develop leaders rather than lead followers (Maxwell, 2002).

Suburban Perspective

Real vs. Perceived Community

Smalltown America during the 1960s and 1970s was the perceived utopian place to grow up. These communities were populations with upper-middle class standards of living that had similar community values, communities were self-sufficient, and everyone knew everyone else and their daily routines. These were the good old days of middle class America in the suburbs. For the most part, these types of communities are the anomaly today, not the norm in suburbia. Census data and the overall changing demographics of all of America show that we are becoming less and less homogeneous. In fact, according to the demographic statistics from 1995, approximately 75 percent of the population was White. The new projected change from this number by the year 2050 will drop 229 percent to 5.39 percent White. That means "other" ethnic and racial groups, including Blacks, Hispanics, Asians and American Indians, will go from 25 percent (in 1995) to 47 percent by 2050. Among those subgroups, Hispanics will be the fastest growing subgroup accounting for approximately 25 percent of the entire U.S. population by 2050 (J. Johnson, 2004).

The impact of these statistics has in recent years become hot political fodder as the debate on how national and even local governments should be handling the significant increase in illegal citizens in our country. The suburbs have not been immune to this influx and so the national issues associated with these changes also are key elements even in local political races. These demographic shifts now set the stage for internal as well as external issues, which the current school administrator in a suburban setting must deal with head-on over the next 10 to15 years.

Internal Politics – Don't Assume Anything

In a recent research-based book on qualities of effective teaching, the author provides a list of positive qualities of effective teachers that is broken down into different student characteristics. Under the student group of "At-Risk Students" (among which there are many diverse populations), the author provides a list of positive teaching qualities and a list of ineffective teaching qualities with this group of students. It is interesting to read the list of both effective and ineffective teaching qualities for teachers in that it appears obvious that members of our own profession haven't yet accepted the fact that all students, regardless of their background, are their responsibility to help in the learning process. For instance, in the positive, effective list, "getting to know the students' culture" is listed, and conversely on the ineffective list is the belief that "students cannot overcome familial and societal issues" (Strong, 2007).

How can a school administrator and leader stand up for equal and improved evaluation to a local, state, or even national audience if his/her own teaching staff believes that a student's background will make all the difference in that child's ability to learn? In addition, teachers then will not even attempt to help that child. In other words, if the political bent of our own teachers is that those of diverse backgrounds start out behind and will stay behind despite what we do in the classroom, then we as administrators need first to deal with this internal problem. Equity, equality, and improvement in our educational system starts with the entire organization believing that all children can learn, despite the baggage, conditions or statures they bring to our doors. Perhaps that is the first political battle we as administrators must deal with in the near future before we too aggressively tackle the state and federal issues surrounding diversity. We must

get our own teaching horses in order in regards to how our teachers perceive the diverse student population.

External Politics – From City Ordinances to NCLB

Local Responses

Most suburban school settings are affiliated with a town or city that
interacts closely with the schools. That small town or city's local media
usually has a reporter that covers the municipal beat and in many cases
also covers school news. When state test scores are publicized and the
results show a shift downward or remain unchanged, the natural response
from the public is that it is due to the new minority population in town
who have pulled the scores down.

City and town officials respond to such generic claims with the typical
politician's response, telling the local patrons that they will look into that
and see what they can do to "fix" the problem. This can and does in many
suburban settings set up an adversarial role between school leaders and
local politicians. The push from politicians to resolve the issue is due to
the economic pressure they feel from merchants and workers who claim
that the scores are a reflection of the changing negative population that
has infiltrated the formerly homogeneous city or town, which they say
is tweaking the economic stability of the town. The school leader, who
is trying to support all students and create an equitable and equal educational opportunity for every child regardless of their background, race,
or origin, can be caught in the middle of a political debate in such small
communities.

The best solution in such situations is to educate those local officials
as to the significant progress such minority students are making, despite

the fact that they may not yet have met a student, and to emphasize the value of diversity in a school setting for all children. The school administrator who keeps his/her community informed of the facts of education and challenges those perceived notions with data can make a significant difference in that community. Hopefully, by challenging prejudice and erroneous assumptions that may be made about minority populations in a small town setting, the administrator must overcome such wrongful assumptions by educating the entire community.

State and Federal Responses

The school administrator's role in supporting and in improving educational opportunities for students in a diverse school setting doesn't stop at the local level. Current budgetary reductions across the U.S. in state funding of education and a significant lack of sufficient funding from the federal level to educate all students require that today's educational leader become a lobbyist for educational support dollars. It is incumbent upon such educational leaders to contact their state and federal legislators and present their case in specifics as to how additional funding can impact improving educational opportunities for diverse student population groups.

Specific program funding from the federal government such as Title I, Title III, and Title V, have provided some ancillary support for educational program needs of diverse student groups, but overall they have not been sufficient to adequately supply what is truly needed. More and more, school administrators have to seek additional funding outside these normal revenue sources. Budgetary line items for staff development, additional support personnel, extended school days, and supplemental curriculum materials are among the most critical items that need to be increased in order to support improved educational opportunities for diverse student groups. If these needs are not met, then improvement in student achievement for our diverse student populations will be very difficult if not impossible to accomplish. The school administrator in a diverse school population setting must be an advocate for state and federal support as well as becoming resourceful in seeking other means of support in order to provide sufficient funding for needed program elements that will serve the diverse student population.

Urban Perspective

According to Webster's *New Collegiate Dictionary*, being political means "the ability to influence others in multiple ways, i.e., "shrewdness in managing people, programs or activities; collaborating with others to achieve a goal or outcome; or effectively dealing with others to achieve a certain agenda, production or desired objective."

The Superintendent's position and function is totally political. The urban educational setting is inundated with politics. Politics impact all areas of district operations. A look at four areas of urban education illustrates the impact of politics. They are 1) federal laws and mandates; 2) state laws and mandates; 3) local elections, expectations and promises; and 4) operational interactions, practices and relationships. The federal laws and mandates clearly create political conditions and impacts on urban schools. The state laws and mandates dictate boundaries, expectations, and accountability assessments for urban districts. The states are assigned the responsibility for educating their children by the Constitution of the United States. The local political role is primarily acted out by school boards, and the operational politics are involved in the daily leadership of the school district.

The Federal Role

The federal role is small for most school districts, but for urban districts, the role is essential for successful operations. The federal impact is felt directly through the Elementary Secondary Education Act (ESEA). A major piece of this law is the "No Child Left Behind (NCLB) Law." The ESEA Law provides supplemental educational services for children of poverty and others in need of support in Language Arts (Reading) and Mathematics. Children in need of support with English as a Second

Language are also helped by ESEA programs. These ESEA programs are commonly called "Title Programs." The most well known of these is the Title I Program, but there are other very important Title programs the district leader must investigate to insure all the dollars available are utilized. The NCLB Law requires a portion of Title I dollars to be used for Supplemental Education Support (SES) programs for students in schools that fail to achieve Adequate Yearly Progress (AYP). Title dollars can be used for preventable intervention for students from impoverished conditions to enable them to be ready for schooling. Title dollars can also be used to support staff development and training for teachers who work to supplement the education of Title students in Language Arts and Mathematics. Title money cannot be used to supplant regular general educational funds, expenses, and obligations.

Federal dollars are also utilized to support the Individuals with Disabilities Education Act (IDEA). This act assists local school districts with the cost of meeting the federal law's requirements for IDEA. The costs of the IDEA mandates are expensive and expansive. Some suburban districts might be able to meet the needs of all students without federal funds, but many rural and almost all urban districts need the federal funds. Urban districts commonly have large Special Education Programs. It is common to have 10 percent to 20 percent of urban students classified as needing some Special Education services. These eligible students make up a wide range of classifications from mild to severe impairments, which include mental, physical, and speech and language services. Urban districts employ a large number of central and building certified and support staff personnel to meet the needs of students. IDEA funds cannot supplant regular district general operating fund dollars, but they are essential for interventions, programs, staff development, and special placement services.

Another major federal support for urban districts is the National School Lunch Program from the Department of Agriculture. This program provides free meals and reduced priced meals for students with low or no family income. The program provides food for breakfast, lunch, and even special summer lunches for students. This federal program assists the urban school districts tremendously by allowing them to operate food programs that do not compromise the funds needed for the instructional program.

Once a district accepts funds from the federal government, it accepts all of the requirements, regulations, mandates, and politics connected to the funds. This is also true for urban schools that participate in the National School Lunch Program. It is almost impossible to find an urban district that does not participate in the ESEA programs, Title programs, the IDEA programs, and/or the National School Lunch program because money in urban districts is limited and many programs face deficits. Urban districts need all of the financial help possible. This common need for operational funds opens the door for federal politics in a major way. You simply can't take the money and refuse to follow the rules of the game. In the total sum of things, urban districts would be at a major disadvantage to meet the expanding needs of their children without federal support. It has become an operational necessity for urban schools to seek federal funds for operations.

Federal programs are strongly influenced by the political party in the majority in the United States House of Representatives, the United States Senate, and the president. This is the ultimate political involvement, and communications with your federal representatives and senators is essential. There are also national advocate organizations that represent the views of those organizations, e.g., The American Association of School

Administrators (AASA), which is the superintendents' organization; The National School Boards Association (NSBA), the School Boards' organization; the National Education Association (NEA), the National Teachers' organization; and many others. There are no greater politics than federal politics; however, we must always remember former House Speaker Tip O'Neal's words, "All politics are local." Politics always start and end at the local level.

President George W. Bush demonstrated the power and influence of the president on federal education law when his party had the majority in the House and Senate. He was the driving force behind the inclusion of the No Child Left Behind Law in the Elementary Secondary Education School Act. The law completely changed the focus on K-12 public education in the United States. Urban school districts are captured by actions and mandates of the federal government because of their dependency on federal funds to meet the needs of urban children.

The State's Role in District Politics

The state's political role is clear. It has the duty to provide a public education program for its children. Often the most challenging part of this role is the demands of the urban communities. The state's governmental bodies, from the governor's office to the Senate and the House of Representatives, are keenly aware of the urban issues, concerns, costs and liabilities.

Urban superintendents must develop a formal and an informal relationship with the state legislators and the governor. The cost of a legislative lobbyist is a necessary expense for the urban school districts. Urban districts must be aware of laws, regulations, and concerns generated daily from the state legislatures. This is very true when they are in session and too often the case when they are out of session. Urban districts need representatives to attend committee hearings, summer study committee meetings, to meet with legislators, meet with representatives of other school districts, and keep informed of political "new ideas" from other states that might be coming their way.

The National Governors' Association has played a key role in getting state governors to assume greater responsibility and leadership of K-12 public education in their states. There are more "Education Governors" than ever before. However, states do not have a common standard for supporting public education. They vary a great deal. Some states fund early childhood education and full day kindergarten. Others have no early childhood programs and barely or poorly fund half-day kindergarten. However, the governors believe that they have to lead public education in their states. They frequently do this by working with the legislature and the state superintendent of education. It is vitally important for urban school superintendents to communicate with the governors of their states, their state superintendent of education, and members of the state legislature. It is important for state politicians to think of the challenges faced by urban superintendents and to seek input from urban superintendents on important issues and concerns pertaining to urban education. It does not matter if the politicians' parties are different. Lines of communication are needed even when the parties are different and issues are disagreeable. The urban superintendents' party is the party of children interest, needs, and welfare. No political philosophy should ever compromise the education of the children.

Urban districts are often depending on the states for funding support. State legislators develop and implement state funding formula that dictates how state dollars are distributed to school districts. It is essential to have lines of communication open to legislators who administer this process. It is vital to share input and testimony at state budget hearing meetings. Always be prepared to share the urban story with the movers and decision makers in the House and Senate budget development process. Most state budget development processes are known by many, but understood by a very few. Get to know the process and, just as critical, get to know those who truly know and understand the state budget process. This is more than understanding the funding formula. Most administrators are knowledgeable about the formula, know the formula, and — just as important — know the process and the people facilitating the process.

Urban superintendents should establish communications with the governors of their states, working to create a relationship with the governors and leading educational representatives. Educational representatives communicate directly with the governors and can make or disregard urban educational concerns. Governors want to be successful and they fully understand who votes for or against them. It is in their personal, political, and professional interest to listen to the concerns, needs, and interest of urban superintendents. Their time is valuable and limited. It is wise to avoid presenting a list of items for consideration. Select one truly important issue and comprehensively make the best case for action. Governors understand the many challenges of leading an urban school district, but why should the urban superintendents problem have a vested interest for them? Connect the dots for them. They may care, but why should they act on the matter? The integrity of the request will be determined by how it is presented by the superintendents or their designees. Always remember that the first meeting sets the urgency and importance of the next meeting. The urban school districts represent the greatest voter diversity in local, state, and national politics. Governors are always seeking ways to bring greater diversity of support to their party and campaigns. Helping to improve urban schools is a powerfully positive political statement that parents, patrons, and average citizens can understand. This point is never lost on wise politicians.

The Local Role in District Politics

The United States Constitution delegated the education of children to the states. The states fulfill this duty by assigning the primary duty of educating students to local governing agencies called boards of education. Local school boards are responsible for establishing schools and, if needed, a system of schools to educate its children. The school boards develop policies to regulate and operate schools, and employs personnel to carry out policy and school operations. A common practice is to employ an executive or superintendent to run the schools. In a few communities in the United States, superintendents are elected by the local citizens, but most communities and school boards employ a person to serve as superintendent.

State law determines the size of school attendance areas or districts. Some districts cover an entire county. Others cover a designated geographic area. But politics are built into state, national, and local school operations. In the early years, a trustee might be elected or appointed to run the local schools, but as populations grew and progress expanded, these trustees gave way to local boards. Some of these boards were appointed by mayors, city councils and other bodies. However, appointed boards gave way to elected boards. General elected boards gave way to boards that represented various areas of the school districts. Now it is common to have boards composed of representatives from specific areas or districts and at-large members from any area. It is important to have designated areas represented because all areas need a voice on the board. Boards that are all at-large are often dominated by persons from a limited represented population.

The basic makeup of local boards ensures politics in education. In urban areas, it is important to have the school system broken down into several board districts. Each district elects at least one member to the school board. Depending upon the size of the school board, five members or seven members or more, there is often a limit placed on the representatives from any one district. This ensures some degree of balance and fairness. It also creates diversity in representation needed to serve a diverse urban community.

To be elected to local school boards, candidates must conduct political campaigns. This process forces school board candidates to be political before they become board members. As the Webster definition for politics says, "The ability to influence others in multiple ways..." Sometimes promises are made verbally and/or tacitly. The campaign makes board candidates available to entertain wants, needs, concerns, and wishes of the voters. The dynamics of campaigning, the acts of communicating their views, expectations, and visions make them political.

Many local school board candidates seek office because they want to make a positive contribution to the community by helping to improve the education of children. A few candidates run because being a school board member is a good "first step" toward higher political office. If a member is successful at this level, there could be a natural progression to city council, mayor, state or higher office. Some seek the school board office because they have a cause or issue that they are determined to correct. All the reasons are political, and board members who depend on voters to elect them to office are political beings. Politics is the definition of campaigning and human interaction.

The challenge of urban superintendents is to convert these school board politicians into school board members who must often set politics aside to do their jobs. From politicians who are school board members to school board members who must be politicians, that is the task. The children and what is best for the school district have to come before getting re-elected or keeping that promise for that group or parents, or an organization. It is impossible to eliminate politics from the school board job, but it is possible to prioritize the job, as much as possible, away from the struggles of politics.

One of the greatest tragedies of local school board politics is the often short tenure of urban superintendents. The 2008 average job life of an urban superintendent is three years. This short superintendent job period compromises reform efforts, creates instability, leadership dysfunctionality, and projects a negative impression of the school district. Dr. Rudy Crew was selected as the 2008 American Association of School Administrators' (AASA) National Superintendent of the Year. He earned the honor for improving education in Miami Dade County, Florida, the fourth largest school system in the country. His school district was a finalist for the prestigious Board Prize for Urban Education, which recognizes the most improved urban school system in the country. Under Crew's watch, Miami Dade's 353,000 student district narrowed the achievement gap among Hispanic children and their White classmates in reading and math at all grade levels. In 2008, Miami Dade's low income Black and Hispanic students outperformed their peers in Florida districts serving students with

similar income levels. About 17,000 more students took advanced placement courses, up from the 13,500 before Crew arrived. The district halved
the number of F-rated schools and earned an overall "B" grade from the
state. This is up from a "C" grade the year before Crew's tenure started.
The number of "A" schools rose from 142 to 171 based upon results from
statewide mandated testing.

So what happened? Beyond the academic improvement, Dr. Crew was
accused of mismanaging the district's $5.5 billion budget and spending its
reserves. He was accused of negligence, insubordination and other offenses.
The real situation emanated from the local politics. Crew never really hit
it off with the powerful Cuban-American community. The relationship
went badly early when Crew rejected demands form the Cuban-American
representatives to remove from district school libraries a children's book,
Vamos a Cuba, which painted a positive picture of life in Cuba. This is the
same Cuba that many Cuban Americans escaped during and after the rev-
olution. Because he failed to pull the book, he became a target for angry
Cuban exiles on Miami Cuban radio. A Hispanic school board member
severely attacked Crew's proposal to balance the budget by reducing
spending on bilingual education at a public school board meeting. Crew,
angry with the member's comments, responded, "Do not talk to me like
a dog!" Monthly board meetings were televised on a board-owned public
TV station, and they became "must see" television for the public. One
drama after another played out. These included board members walking
out, public speakers being escorted out by security guards. Racial issues
surfaced in 2006 when Crew filed an ethics complaint against a white
Cuban-American member of the Florida House of Representatives for
using racial epithets in English and Spanish to describe Crew, an African
American. This representative had to resign from the legislature over the

scandal. This really compromised Crew's relations with state lawmakers, especially Republicans.

Local politics, race, legal battles, money, and change created a severe storm in Miami-Dade's school system. Rudy Crew was the initial victim of the storm, but the biggest losers were the children. Crew created changes that resulted in improved education for children, but the politics were too great for him to survive. Judy Rizzo, executive director of the James B. Hunt, Jr. Institute for Educational Leadership and Policy in Durham, North Carolina, told Crew early on to "Be mindful of the politics. You're the wrong color in this town." She said, "In most urban school districts, nine out of ten kids are Black. In Miami, it's different. The power structure is different." One board member said Crew created too much turmoil and negativity in the community. Crew said, "Miami politics is immature."

There are many aspects to Rudy Crew's adventures in Miami-Dade's County School System. However, it is a good example of local politics and how very powerful their consequences can become.

The Operational Role and Politics

Politics are everywhere. When people interact, politics are created. In administering and supervising the daily operations of an urban school district, politics are routinely integrated in the process. Almost every decision an administrator makes is loaded with political implications. Every decision creates winners and losers or creates those who benefit more than others. The best means of living with politics in operating the urban school district is to effectively and clearly communicate expectations, rules, guidelines, policies, and who will be held accountable.

Operational politics are prevalent from the top of the district, at the board and superintendent level, down to the school support personnel. The largest political overt indicator of politics is how people perceive they are being treated. Treating people in a positive manner that is invitational and open is the most effective practice. However, there is no such thing as 100 percent equality of relationships, opportunities, and operations. There are indeed "different strokes for different folks." In general, there should be little observable differences. In diverse working environments, special efforts must be taken to improve communications and relationships among employees. There are many laws governing many of the politics of local operations. Laws protecting against violations based on age, race, sex, and ethnic discrimination are in place to help us regulate the politics of local operations.

Chapter 3 Case Studies

Case Study 1: Urban

You are the superintendent of an urban school district. The parents for a Quality School Board come to you with a concern. They have been looking for good candidates for your school board and they are not sure if their list of possible board members would be good for you. They want you to sit down with them and review the list of candidates and pick the members who could best help you lead the district. They must get their list cut from seven candidates to three before the end of the week. They need your help as soon as possible and they are willing to meet with you at a place and time of your choice. What will you do?

Case Study 2: Suburban

A local group of parents from Northeast High School are very angry with their principal and they want her dismissed from her job at the end of the current school year. They had numerous issues with the principal during the first semester of the year. However, what she did during the last days before the Christmas Break was the last straw. Mrs. Jones, the Principal, refused to allow a group of African American students to attend the inauguration of President-elect Barack Obama. African Americans make up 60 percent of Northeast High School and parents demanded that they be allowed to be part of history. Mrs. Jones, the Principal, allowed a group of white Jewish students to visit the Holocaust Museum during Fall Break, and the students were allowed to receive extra credit for the activity. There are no Black girls on the Northeast Cheerleading Team, and that includes freshmen, reserve, and varsity teams. You are the African

American superintendent of this school district and these parents demand action. It is now the first week back to school in January. The inauguration is in three weeks. What will you do?

Case Study 3: Rural

Many school leaders shift from leader to manager, and may develop strength in one of these roles. As a small-school leader this shift in roles may be a necessity. As a small- school superintendent, determine which of the following duties you will perform yourself or delegate to a subordinate. Circle the letter of the following rating scale to make the determination:

    A = I will keep the assignment for myself

    B = I will delegate to a principal

    C = I will delegate to a clerical person in my office

A B C   Provide in-service to teachers to increase their effectiveness.

A B C   Supervise the job performance of custodial, clerical or other support staff.

A B C   Plan, develop and implement a process for student, teacher, and parental involvement in determining curriculum goals and objectives.

A B C   Organize a system for dealing with discipline issues.

A B C   Assign teachers and paraprofessional staff to classrooms.

A B C   Arrange transportation for students to extracurricular activities.

A B C   Ensure that approved budget monies are received.

A B C   Recruit applicants for vacant positions.

A B C   Monitor the expenditure of funds raised by booster clubs, student activities or other community groups.

A B C   Patrol the parking lot.

Chapter 4

Funding

Rural Perspective

General Information

Funding for rural school districts is quite simple and can be divided into three categories: federal funds, state funds, and local funds. Additional federal and state funding may be obtained through competitive grants; however, for the traditional rural school, the financial stability rests on the level of federal, state and local revenue.

Federal funding for the rural district in which this author serves is categorized as Title IA, IIA, IID, III, IV and V. The largest of the federal fund categories is Title IA. The funds from this category are designed to assist in educational services for the economically disadvantaged. Another federal funding category designed to meet the special needs of students is Individuals with Disabilities Education Act, or IDEA.

School district revenue obtained through state funding in Oklahoma is calculated through a state funding formula. This formula is designed to provide financial equity to all schools within the state. The formula uses certain factors such as local property taxes and revenue obtained for taxation of local industry to calculate the amount of state revenue per district.

On the local level, school district revenue is based on local property taxes. Oklahoma is one of only a few states who depend on the taxation of local land owners as the primary source of revenue for common education.

Explanation of State Aid

As stated previously, state aid is calculated according to a formula. To a new school board member or a new administrator, there is perhaps no term more mysterious than "the formula." The term is bandied about by those who know, or think they know—much to the consternation of those who do not. In trying to fathom the term, visions may arise of a mad scientist mixing up a secret formula in a vat in the basement of the state capitol in which educational dollars are immersed, only to emerge with a different status.

To begin the discussion of state aid, suppose you are a member of the legislature and you have to decide how to distribute education funds to 500 school districts, which are rural and urban, rich and poor, declining and growing, large and small. What factors will you use in determining how much each district receives? Certainly giving equal amounts to each district would be preposterous because either the large districts would be starved or the small districts would be awash in funds. You could distribute funds based on the physical size of the district—so many dollars for each square mile. But a square mile in western Oklahoma may not contain any students as compared to a square mile in Tulsa that contains 100 students per square mile. Distribution based on area would not be a fair funding criterion either. You could allot funds based on district population—so much money per resident. But district populations are not always readily known, and some districts, such as those located along eastern lakes, might contain far more retirees than the average district, while those located in suburbs might have far more school-aged children than the average district.

One could give each district the exact amount that particular district needed. But by the time such a lengthy individualized process could be completed, the school year would be over. Such a procedure, even if it could be done, thus would not be practical.

However, there is one statistic that is known and which is certainly relevant to educational costs: the number of students attending each school district. For that reason, the basis of state funding is the apportionment of money to school districts based upon student enrollment.

A "formula" (a series of steps used in driving a district's state aid) was created because districts are different—they vary in student population, student characteristics, and fixed costs in educating those students. The formula seeks to account for the broad student variables between districts.

Basing educational funds on the number of students attending a school district is just the starting point for devising a funding formula. The premise that differences in students are relevant to education costs, and therefore to what funds a district should receive, is generally accepted because some students cost more to educate than do others. This is where the concept of "weights" arises—that it is not equitable to give funds solely on the basis of attendance because student needs and the costs to meet those needs vary between districts due to certain known factors. Since students in some categories cost more to educate than students outside those categories, a district with more students fitting into the set categories should receive more state aid than it would if it did not have those students.

The first relevant category is the age of the students. It costs more to educate some grade levels than it does others. It would not be fair to give a district that has students congregated in the grades that cost more the same funds per student as is given to a district that has students congregated more in the grades that cost less to educate. Therefore, "weights" have been assigned by the legislature to different grade levels; the higher the weight, the more money that will be received by the district for educating that student. For example, in 1999-2000, each student in grades 4, 5, and 6 was given a grade level weight of 1.0, while each student in grades 7 through 12 was given a weight of 1.2. These weights mean that junior high and high school students are generally recognized as costing 20 percent more to educate that are fourth, fifth, and sixth grade students. The students assigned the greatest weights are in grades 1 and 2, who are given a weight of 1.351. The students assigned the least weights are early childhood education students, who receive a weight of 0.7.

Age or grade level is not the only broad variable relevant to education costs and to the funding a district should receive to pay for those costs. A second grade with 20 students, 10 of whom have hearing or sight problems, will cost more to educate than will a second grade with 20 students who have no handicapping conditions. Recognizing that expenses increase for certain students, there are "student category weights" that relate to disabilities. The greatest weight, 3.8, is assigned to "deaf and blind" and "visually impaired" students. Thus, a fourth grade visually impaired student's weight is 4.8 (1.0 grade level weight and 3.8 category weight); a second grade "hearing impaired" student's weight is 4.251 (1.351 grade level weight and 2.9 category weight).

Explanation of Formula

The "formula" that determines a district's state aid is: State Aid = Foundation Aid + Transportation Supplement. Note that there is an "initial" state aid calculation in July and a "final" state aid calculation in December. Districts are to be notified of the initial allocation by July 15 and the final allocation by January 15.

A. FOUNDATION AID

The first portion of the formula determines the district's foundation aid. The first step in determining foundation aid is calculating the district's students' weights, which is called the district's "weighted average daily membership" (ADM). The final foundation program is the district's highest weighted ADM based on the first nine weeks of the current school year, the preceding school year, or the second preceding school year. Three weights are assigned to foundation aid:

1. The weighted pupil grade level calculation;

2. The weighted pupil category calculation; and

3. The weighted district calculation.

a. The Weighted Pupil Grade Level Calculation

ADM is multiplied by the weights given to each grade to determine the district's total weight for all grades. Remember, the grade level weight for grades 4 through 6 is 1.0. If the ADM for these grades is 100, the grade level weight for these grades is 100. If the ADM for grades 7 through 12 is 200, then the weight for these grades is 240 (1.2 x 200). The weights for each grade level are added, and the total is the "weighted pupil grade level calculation."

b. Weighted Pupil Category Calculation

This calculation involves multiplying the number of pupils in the preceding school year by the weights statutorily assigned each category, and then adding the totals. If the number of visually impaired students is 10, the weight for this category is 38 (10 x 3.8).

c. Weighted District Calculation

This part of the formula concerns a "small school district formula" and a "district sparsity-isolation formula," using whichever formula produces the greatest number. The "small school district formula" applies only to districts whose highest ADM of the preceding two years is less than 529 students.

The "district sparsity-isolation formula" applies only to districts whose total number of square miles exceeds the average number of square miles of all districts and whose density is less than one-fourth of the state's average "areal" density. Area density is determined by dividing ADM by the district's total area in square miles.

If a district qualifies, the formula is calculated by multiplying the district student cost factor by the district's area factor and then multiplying this figure by ADM. The resulting number is counted as additional students.

The district's student cost factor is found by categorizing ADM into grade level groups of K-5, 6-8, and 9-12 and arriving at a figure after multiplying, dividing, and adding certain statutorily-set numbers and fractions. The weighted district calculation may be reduced if, after the calculations are applied, the district's projected per-pupil revenue exceeds 150 percent of the projected state average per-pupil revenue.

Further, state aid that a district is calculated to receive as a result of the weighted district calculation is reduced if the district's carryover funds of the most recent fiscal year data available, plus state aid generated by the weighted district calculation, exceed certain percentages of the district's general fund.

In review, foundation aid is determined by adding the district's student weights, those being:

1. The grade level weights (ADM times the weights given for students in each grade);

2. The pupil category weights (ADM times the weights given for disabled, gifted, economically disadvantaged, and bilingual students); and

3. The weighted district calculation, if applicable.

The total of these weights is multiplied by the amount of money the legislature has designated as "foundation support level income." If the support level is $1,000 and the district's total weighted ADM is 732.62, then the district's state foundation support level is $732,620. But, there is another part of the formula that is applied before determining the amount of foundation aid: the subtraction of "chargeable" from the "foundation program." A chargeable is thus a deduction from the first determined dollar amount in the foundation aid formula—the foundation program. The chargeables are called "foundation program income." Chargeables mainly include:

a. The adjusted assessed district valuation in the current school year, minus the previous year's protested ad valorem tax revenues held as prescribed by the state law, multiplied by 15 miles;

b. 75% of the County Four Mill levy proceeds received during the preceding fiscal year; and

c. Amount received from School Land earnings, gross production tax receipts, motor vehicle collection, and REA tax.

After subtracting these totals, we have finally arrived at your district's foundation aid, which is:

1. The district's total student weights times the foundation support figure set by the legislature, minus

2. The total of the chargeable.

Note: The July calculation of per-pupil revenue is determined by dividing the district's second preceding year's total weighted ADM into the district's second preceding year's total revenues excluding certain receipts. The December calculation of per-pupil revenue is determined by dividing the district's preceding year's total weighted ADM into the district's preceding year's total revenues excluding certain receipts.

B. SALARY INCENTIVE AID

The journey to determine state aid has cleared one important hurdle, but it is not over. Having determined foundation aid, one must now calculate the district's "salary incentive aid." Salary incentive aid is in part designed to help districts that pay a higher proportion of teachers' salaries than do the average school districts. A teacher minimum salary schedule has been set by law, and each district must pay at least the amount prescribed. Because the minimum salary schedule pays more to teachers who have more experience and pays more to teachers who have earned advanced degrees, districts employing many veteran teachers with advanced degrees will have higher salary costs than districts employing teachers of relatively little experience and few advanced degrees. Incentive aid tries to help those districts employing more veteran teachers and teachers with more advanced degrees to offset in part the higher costs for employing those teachers. An average state district teacher to which each school district's teacher staff is compared is determined from information submitted to the state department by each district. The information is received from the teacher personnel report, which lists the years of teaching experience and degree of every teacher in each district.

A district's personnel report is the basis for determining each district's weighted average district teacher. The weights for teachers are set by statute. For example, a teacher with a bachelor's degree and 0-2 years of experience is multiplied by .7, while a teacher with a doctor's degree and more than 15 years of experience is multiplied by 1.6. If a district's average teacher weight is more than the state's weighted average state teacher amount, then that district qualifies for salary incentive aid. The difference between the state average weighted teacher and a district's average weighted teacher is called the "district teacher index." This index is multiplied by a factor set by law, currently 7, and this figure is called the "district teacher factor." This teacher factor is in turn multiplied by the sum of the district's weighted pupil grade level calculation and weighted pupil category calculation.

ADM is also used to determine weights in the salary incentive formula. After the use of these weights and various multipliers, the department calculates a district's "total weighted ADM." Salary incentive aid includes additional amounts to encourage district voters to approve school millage by paying districts a set dollar amount for each mill levied above 15 mills for each weighted ADM. Since districts approve all 35 mills of local school millage, districts will have 20 mills applied to the calculation. The salary incentive aid formula calculation includes:

    a. Multiplying your district's Total Weighted ADM (let's say it is 500) times an Incentive Aid Guarantee Factor (say, $60) ($30,000);

b. Subtracting from the amount 1/1000 of the district's assessed valuation (say $2,000,000), ($2.000); and,

c. Multiplying that amount ($28,000) by the amount of mills levied above 15 (which would be 20 – the County Four Mill Levy not counting). The district's Salary Incentive Aid is thus $560,000.

C. TRANSPORTATION SUPPLEMENT

The formula has one more step to hurdle, that being the "transportation supplement." This part of the formula is determined by multiplying the "average daily haul"—the daily average number of pupils legally transported in the district who live more than one and one half miles from school—times the "per capita allowance" times the "transportation factor." The per capita allowance is a dollar amount based upon district density (the lower density of students, the higher the allowance). The transportation factor is a number set by the legislature.

The sum of the foundation aid, the salary incentive aid, and the transportation supplement is the district's state aid.

Suburban Perspective

No matter in which setting (urban, suburban, or rural) an administrator is working, historically, the primary funding sources for supporting diverse student programs have come from federal dollars, with the most popular dollars coming from Title I, Title III, and Title II funds. Each of these federal programs is targeted to provide funding to supplement local and state funding so that where concentrations of specific sub-populations are within a school district, these dollars can be utilized. Despite the positive intent of each of these federal support programs, there are issues with such funding. The two that are most problematic are the overall inadequacy of this funding and the restrictive controls on how these needed dollars can be spent at the local level for these subgroups.

Title I

The focus of Title I support funds is for students demonstrating a low academic performance who are children of poverty. The method whereby that poverty is determined is the socio-economic status of the district. This is most frequently determined by the percentage of students who are receiving free and reduced lunch on the federal lunch program. In most cases, the districts with the higher percentages of low socio-economic status receive more federal money than those who have a lower percentage of students in the federally subsidized lunch program. Amounts per child may vary state to state as this money is distributed to the states as a "block grant" program. The most positive aspect of Title I funding in a suburban district that may be receiving the funds is that it can be utilized in the target areas of the district where the greatest academic need is seen for this low socio-economic group. The most negative aspect, on the other hand, especially in a suburban setting where there may be a fairly low or average percentage of low (SES) students, is that the funds are usually not sufficient to meet the entire district's targeted needs.

Title III

Title III funds provide federal assistance for school districts that have students who are entering our schools without having English as their daily operational language. Across the United States, pockets of non-English speaking students can vary in the native language these students bring to various suburban districts. In some districts, a single language such as Spanish may be the dominant or sole native language of these non-English speaking students. In other suburban settings, especially in those school districts that may be immediately adjacent to large urban areas, there may be multiple ethnic groups and multiple languages spoken by that district's non-English speaking students. Regardless of the number of different languages spoken by non-English speaking students, the funding supports from Title III are to be focused on ensuring that they have programmatic elements of their instruction that will help them become fluent speakers of English in order to function and succeed in the all-English school setting and to eventually graduate as an English speaker. Once again, this federal block grant distributed to the states will vary in its per-student support in various locations around the country. Like Title I, the larger dollars from Title III come to districts who have a higher number of students who do not speak English as their native language. In suburban settings where there may be just a handful of students who are identified as non-English speaking, these per-student dollars from Title III are usually either non-existent or not worth the effort on the part of the district to receive because they won't provide enough program support for much of anything of value to assist the district in improving their non-English speaking curriculum.

Title II

This federal grant provides for training for faculty. It can be important to school districts with diverse populations because the money it provides can be specifically targeted to the training of teachers who support those diverse students in the classroom. Once again, insufficient dollars in this category of funding is the common problem in school districts, but it at least can provide extra training opportunities for areas like differentiation, literacy assessment, developmental reading, and other targeted teacher training needs to support students of diverse backgrounds.

Other Sources

Although these federal grants are the largest and most common support mechanisms for funding programs for diverse student populations, other sources exist and can be sought by administrators. There are limited competitive federal grants (like Century 21) and private grant opportunities. In addition, local and state grant sources can also be pursued by school districts to provide supplemental assistance for programs to support diverse student populations. The administrators in suburban districts who find their coffers insufficient to provide quality program offerings for their diverse populations must not only become more creative users of existent monies, but active seekers of these alternative grants. Pursuing such monies in larger districts usually falls under the role of grant writers or specific administrators assigned the job of seeking such extra funding sources. In most suburban school settings, such a position usually doesn't exist and is either an added job of the central office administration or is assigned to an already overburdened building administrator. In summary, when the regular channels of funding aren't enough to pay for the program, the good administrators become resourceful and seek those extra dollars creatively.

Hopeful Future

In recent discussions among federal education officials in Title I, there seems to be a more accepting understanding of the need to broaden the use of the Title I monies. This would apply to other categorical groups such as non-English speaking students. As all federal funding becomes harder to acquire, relaxing these previous restrictions among these grants may be the administrator's only hope of adequately providing the support needed for diverse student needs in all types of districts.

Urban Perspective

Funding

One of the primary urban concerns is school funding. The level of funding is commonly below the level of needs and operational expenses. District operational expenses are common in urban, rural, and suburban districts. They involve the operational expenses associated with paying personnel; utility costs; insurance expenses; facility repair and maintenance costs; transportation costs; technology hardware, software, license operational costs; and other costs necessary to conduct a public education school district.

Sources of Revenue

Urban school districts are funded with local, state and minimal federal dollars. The most common sources of funding are property taxes, sales taxes, inventory taxes, vehicle taxes, financial institution taxes, gaming taxes, license excise taxes, innkeepers or hotel taxes, sale taxes and income taxes.

Local Funds:

The local urban school district is often compromised in its ability to maximize on taxes because taxes are often higher in urban communities than they are in suburban and rural communities. Urban taxpayers are subject to added taxable obligations for funding safety, public transportation expenses, health care costs, city services, and public service obligations. These costs are added to school costs, resulting in higher tax costs. These costs are not helped by city tax abatements for developments, special tax breaks for local developments, tax inference financing (TIF), and the loss of tax revenue from high-cost public properties that are tax exempt or completely off the tax rolls. The loss of exempted properties directly reduces the district's assessed valuation and drives up the rate of taxation on urban taxpayers.

State Funds:

State funds are provided to local urban school districts for specific purposes. These funds are used for early childhood programs, kindergarten, special education, pre-school, Limited English Proficiency (LEP), and non-English speaking programs, textbook reimbursement expenses, free and reduced-priced lunches, professional development, state assessment tests and remediation, career and technical education, special education funds, summer school costs, general instructional and operational expenses.

Federal Funds:

Federal funds are funds directed at supporting the Elementary Secondary Education Act, which includes mandates of the No Child Left Behind Law and an assortment of Federal Title programs. Federal funds for the Individuals with Disabilities Education Act (IDEA) are provided for local urban districts. Federal grants for special programs are often available for districts that qualify. The National School Lunch Program also provides needed resources for urban districts to provide an affordable free and reduced-price lunch program.

Other Funds:

Most states allow school districts to apply directly through their communities to raise funds for operations, facility renovations, and new construction. Many communities have to conduct a campaign to increase the tax rate for operations. This amounts to a full-scale political campaign with legal guidelines, specifications and regulations. Other communities conduct referendum campaigns to raise taxes or to sell bonds for school operations, facilities renovations, and new constructions. These are very tough campaigns to conduct in communities with high taxes and low socio-economic living levels. These campaigns are difficult and very challenging in urban school districts.

Communicating the Need

One of the fundamental responsibilities of an urban superintendent is to communicate the district's funding needs to people. Employing a lobbyist at the state legislature is needed to keep on top of each issue, but it is essential, especially important, to get the superintendent with the right legislators to seek help on funding issues. The superintendent must also get out to talk to community groups, pastors, chamber of commerce members, corporate leaders, parent and community groups, and faculty and staff groups about funding needs. It is a good investment of time to speak to service groups, church groups and others about the funding needs of the urban school district. The superintendent should organize community advisory groups or discussion groups to share the message and seek assistance in spreading the message to all sectors of the urban community.

The urban superintendent should be able to rally hundreds of parents and community patrons to attend special meetings, rallies or demonstrations to illustrate the urgency and importance of a concern. This does not occur without a network of supporters and followers. Organization, communication, feedback and action create a viable group of followers and persons willing to help the school district. It is a good idea to include employee groups, unions, ministers, community leaders, retired teachers and administrators and as many parents as possible. Numbers are needed in urban districts to demonstrate the importance of the issue and/or concern. School funding is an issue relevant to employees, parents, community leaders and others.

An essential key to an effective urban school district's communication initiative is to get all the people the same story or common communication points. Every meeting must have a purpose with goals and achievable objectives. The worst possible sin is to waste the time of busy people. Ten small meetings might be more strategic and successful than a large meeting. The large meeting is often the action meeting. It takes time to create an effective responsive action initiative.

Referendum

The urban district's attempt to be successful in a referendum campaign has to occur long before the campaign. Having a need for higher salaries or renovations or construction will not be great enough to overcome the resistance to new or higher taxes. The campaign has to start today.

Public Relations

It is important to get parents, patrons, and others to visit and get involved in the schools. The first activity could be an open house or a Grandparents and Greats Day. It is just important to get people into the schools. Urban schools could allow community groups and organizations to meet in their schools. The point is to get them into the school under positive circumstances. The next step is to create a community roster of parents and patrons and invite them to special school programs. The activities could be open houses, talent shows, plays, award programs, Veterans Day activities, etc.

Create a community school newsletter to snail-mail or send via email. Work to develop a connection between the school and the community patron. This is not a short-term relationship. It takes several years to establish a solid connection and this might not result in one school visitation, but you are building awareness and relations.

Leadership Committee

Each urban school should be able to name two or three parents to serve on a community leadership or school support committee. It is important to work with a group of cooperative parents to get them to exercise leadership in supporting urban schools. This group might be needed to lead a referendum campaign when school officials are prohibited from participating. Even an outside professional consultant will need local parents and patrons to help with a campaign.

Every school principal can play an important role in getting parents involved in a school support committee. This could become a normal expectation of the principal's job duties.

Chapter 4 Case Studies

Case Study 1: Rural

It is evident that you are short by 75K in next calendar year budget. You do have reduction in force policy in your negotiated contract with your certificated staff. There have been no real attempts to analyze line by line the budget. If you cut staff, you must do so right away because there will be only three months worth of savings for the next calendar year. You know you will have an increased influx of Hispanic students next year that you have to serve. Your board still wants you to keep at least a 10% operating balance. You could balance the budget if they will allow you to reduce your operating balance. How will you go about deciding what to do to balance your budget? Give the top five ideas you have to go about meeting the district needs. Be sure to explain why you would make these choices.

Case Study 2: Suburban

Your buildings are all 35-plus years old and in a state of disrepair. Your board has contracted a facility study and has voted to try to do a $56 million project updating the high school and middle school. You are in Indiana and must pass a referendum. There is already opposition to your project because of the economy and the fact that your student make-up is changing demographically and no longer looks as it has in the past. Many of the "old guard" do not want the community make-up to change and feel the projects are being driven by these new students moving into the area. What kinds of facts will you gather to attempt to pass the referendum? How will you be sure the message gets out to the community with the restraints you have by the current state law?

Case Study 3: Urban

The chairperson of the House Ways and Means Committee would like to be responsive to the needs of your urban school district. He has scheduled a meeting of the House Ways and Means Committee and has requested that you come and provide testimony about your financial needs. However, he insists that you be specific with needs, funding, funding amounts and indicators of accountability, and results for funds provided. You will have only 15 minutes for the presentation, followed by questions from the chair and members of the committee. What will you do and how will you focus your presentation in such a short period of time?

Case Study 4: Urban

You have just assumed the superintendent's position in a mid-western urban city. The district has desperate facility needs. There are buildings in need of renovations and facilities beyond repair and in need of new construction. Six months ago, the district's referendum campaign for facilities renovations and construction was defeated by a margin of three to one. The city has only about 40 percent of eligible students in your school district. Develop a strategic plan to successfully pass a facility referendum within the next two years.

Chapter 5

Visioning and Planning
for Improvement

Rural Perspective

Helen Keller was once asked by a reporter if there was anything worse than being blind?
She replied, "Yes, someone with sight but no vision."

It may be easier in a rural setting to become myopic when it comes to diversity. It has been overheard many times by leaders in superintendent gatherings in rural settings that they have little or no diversity in their small corporations. This is, of course, because they are thinking of diversity being only where their students come from, the language they speak and the color of their skin. This narrow view of diversity is often reflected in the vision or lack of vision for these schools. As has been stated many times through this book, there is much more to diversity and meeting diverse needs of stakeholders than this simplistic view.

Even when speaking of poverty, many have too narrow a thought about which students can be affected and how it can impact the diverse needs. Often the simple answer is that our school is or is not a Title school and that defines whether or not there is much poverty that needs to be addressed. The fact is, there are really two types of poverty and the needs for each of these students and families are very different. There is, of course, the financial poverty that many families suffer from and, in most all schools settings, the sitting district leader will have to deal with making sure these students' needs are met. It is often easy to identify these students through federal programs like Title programs and the free and reduced lunch/breakfast programs.

The second type of poverty that is often overlooked and thus under-addressed is that of emotional poverty. These students and families are much harder to identify because, on the surface, they look like they have it all together. They have nice clothes, plenty of food and nice homes.

However, under the surface many of these children and their families are emotionally bankrupt. We see this in the continuing abuse of drugs and alcohol and the destruction of the nuclear family as we know it. The parents are working two jobs to pay for all the "things" they have and the children are left to fend for themselves, and this takes a huge toll on them emotionally. To identify and meet the diverse needs of this group, it takes more time to diagnose and serve the needs of these children. It is much tougher than simply providing the basic staples of life.

What this writer finds interesting is that a family can be financially bankrupt but emotionally wealthy. Likewise they can be both financially and emotionally bankrupt at the same time. In a financially strong family, they can still be emotionally bankrupt and can be hiding the pain behind the trappings of the American lifestyle of success. In a time when many are losing jobs and homes, this group of seemingly well-adjusted students on the outside could be fast approaching the bankrupt status in both the financial and emotional realms.

Saying this, then how does the district leader address the diverse needs of the perceived homogeneous group of students in a rural setting? One answer, of course, is to look at the vision for the school district and the plan to meet the needs of the ever-increasing diverse group of students. Whether the children and families are rich, poor, Caucasian, African-American, Hispanic, Asian, smart, challenged or any other difference, the district leader's job is to be sure an adequate opportunity for a quality educational experience is there for all, even when times and students are changing.

For this writer, "visioning" is an integral part of the overall planning process. Simplistically, a plan should be made up of a vision, mission, goals and objectives. To create this plan, analyses must be completed to see where a school corporation is before an adequate plan can be adopted to meet the perceived needs. This is done in many ways by different facilitators, but keeping the process as simple as possible and the plan as applicable as possible seems to work best.

Some analysis techniques may include a stakeholder analysis, a beliefs audit, and a SWOT (strengths, weaknesses, opportunities, threats) analysis. By doing this, the corporation can identify the diverse needs of all its stakeholders and be sure the vision and plan reflect those diverse needs.

Once the plan has been conceived, it is imperative that an action plan is in place to see the plan come to fruition. The objectives should be measurable and have a timeline connected to them so the corporation and its leadership can continually monitor the progress. Data must be kept on all initiatives, and especially on the specific programs and targets for those students' identified needs through the stakeholder analysis and beliefs audits. What a strong message can be sent to a small community that a diverse group of students have been identified and their needs met through the visioning and planning process.

It is amazing that many corporations still do not do any specific corporate plan with specific vision and mission. They may have a vision statement and/or a mission statement, but there is no specific plan on how to make their school corporation better for their constituents.

There are many positives about leading a small rural corporation. There are also many problems. Diversity or the perceived lack of diversity can be one of the issues in leading a small, seemingly homogeneous corporation. Many of the families will have been in the community for years and will have gone to the same schools their children and grandchildren attend or are attending. The schools become theirs, and changing anything may be a traumatic event in the community. If students from any other culture move in or if there is even a dramatic growth of the student population, the school community can be adversely affected if a solid plan is not in place. The vision for the school and the plan for reaching the vision can be the rudder that holds the corporation on course to meet the needs of all its students.

John Kotter in his book *Eight Stages of Change* states that there must be a sense of urgency before any change can occur. He also says that, to change a culture in an organization, it takes three to five years to engrain the new culture (Kotter, 1999). Both of these facts have been shown to be true in schools where this author has served. A very specific strategic plan with the vision, mission, goals and objectives is an important part of changing a school corporation's culture to be sure all diverse needs of all students are being addressed.

When addressing planning and visioning, there seems to be an issue of whether it should be a long-range plan or a short-term plan; the answer is yes. Especially in a public school there should be both. Our educational environment is changing so rapidly that if we only do a long-range planning process, the issues we face today may never have even been thought of three to five years ago. Some believe a ten-year plan will keep them on track to successfully meeting the diverse needs of their students, but that couldn't be farther from the truth. We should cast the vision out for five to ten years, but we must constantly be revisiting it to be sure we are going down the right path. To do this, an annual plan should be put in place for the school corporation, and each individual school's plan should fit into the vision of the corporation as a whole.

The questions for the district leader should be, who are you serving, what are their needs and how do you meet them? The only way to answer these questions is through a very specific, ever-changing plan with a planning process that enables the district leader to identify and plan to meet the diverse needs of all its stakeholders.

Suburban Perspective

Diversity Equals a Tougher Vision

It would be rare for any person interviewing for a school district leadership position today to not be asked to define their vision for education. School boards, community members, teachers, and fellow administrators want their school leader to be able to define the plan, to set the course for action and improvement, and to be able to clearly articulate it to everyone. In a diverse school setting, there are a few additional issues inherent in the visioning process that make it unique from a district with a homogeneous student population. There is no question that the complexities of learning are difficult to master in any setting, but when you mix in the poverty factor, language barriers, and significant cultural differences, the planning process becomes even more challenging. The fainthearted should not embark on pursuing a leadership role in a district with a diverse student population unless you are ready to be flexible and a student of the change process. There is no way you will be able to establish an effective vision in the diverse school district unless you see the visioning process as a dynamic, ever-changing, and systemic function of your leadership.

The following quotes best explain the perspective required in the process. "Leaders in a culture of change deliberately establish innovative conditions and processes in the first place and they guide them after that" (Fullan, 2001). Pascale advises these new leaders to "design more than engineer, discover more than dictate, and decipher more than presuppose." (Pascale et all, 2000).

Examining these suggested elements of the change process and the actions recommended for leaders is a great starting point for putting the visioning and improvement process in place. The first step is to be innovative in your approach to planning. Put more simply, you'd never see improvements without changing and charting a new course from what has already been done, and from that which hasn't worked before. The successful leader must seek new and innovative ways to attack the issues surrounding diversity. As you plan and establish the corporate vision, it is requisite that the successful leader ensures the methods for improvement are working. This is the dynamic piece of planning and visioning. Too many leaders set the vision through a well-intentioned strategic planning process, but then just sit back and await the outcome, expecting the vision to occur just because it has been declared and agreed to by all. Innovative and creative approaches must be regularly initiated, measured for effectiveness, and constantly assessed to frequently redefine the vision. An example of this would be in a district where the phrase "learning for all" defines a corporate vision. Learning can be defined in many contexts and at different levels. If this vision is to be meaningful and effective, all of the stakeholders in the district must know what is meant by learning in their schools and how we show that learning is happening. They need to see new ideas, measured results, and positive outcomes to believe in that vision. When it has those characteristics, then the vision becomes accepted, shared, and an active force for improvement.

Another more specific example would be monitoring the reading progress of all first graders in a district. In a diverse school setting, the range of reading ability of this group (all first graders) would be extremely wide. The key though to accomplish the stated vision of "learning for all" is to assess growth and improved reading skills, so that even the lowest-scoring student is able to demonstrate progress in reading over time. The dynamic process of making the vision—in this case, "learning for all"—a constant, ever-developing action plan is the key to successfully achieving it.

The educational leader of a diverse school population needs to become, as Pascale and his associates describe, more of a "designer," a "discoverer," and a "decipherer" of the organizational vision as the data is discovered and shared.

Urban Perspective

The average tenure of an urban superintendent in 2008 was three years. This is one of the most important facts to know and consider as an urban superintendent creates visions and plans for improvement. It simply means that the vision has to be sharp and the plans short and immediate. Joe Garcia, Miami-Dade's County school district's former spokesman, said that in one of Superintendent Crew's early planning meetings, Crew drew a sharp arc to illustrate how much work needed to be done in the first year. Garcia said that Crew stated, "… you have to climb the hill fast and hard that first year to get high enough so you have the public support to continue your work." Garcia says, "If you drop below that line of parent-public concern, people start to mess with you. If you stay above it, that's where real improvement starts to happen." Well, this writer has never been in the situation that Rudy Crew found himself in at Miami-Dade's County School System, but I agree with his idea or vision of a fast start and quick climb in the first six months of an urban job. However, there are some fundamental points all potential urban superintendents must know and consider.

Point #1: Vision and Plan

It is important for any superintendent to have a 60- to 90-day entry plan for any new job. However, for an urban superintendent, it is a matter of success or failure. You only get one opportunity to make a good "first impression." Be prepared! Create that short-term vision. Short term is six months or less.

The Short-Term Vision

The short-term vision is built from the research, facts, information, and local feedback about the district, plus your ability to match up with the urgent overt needs of the district. This short-term vision cannot be "blue sky" or a "make a wish" kind of vision. It must be fashioned by a pragmatic knowledge of the current district status quo.

Once the short term vision is solid, an action plan has to be developed with a daily or weekly chronology. This planned chronology becomes your guide for action. Point number one is the win or lose point. You cannot afford to do poorly in this area without some serious repercussions.

Point #2: See and Timing or Prioritize Actions

The time window for change is limited in urban educational superintendent situations. However, Rudy Crew's approach is not appropriate in every urban situation. There are some situations where the 60- to 90-day plan might be to enforce the status quo and to research and study the district. There is no doubt that a good first impression is essential, but that impression could be one of respecting what is there and making plans for improvement. It could be meeting all the players and identifying forces for change or opposition to change. The new superintendent's plan could be more formative than summative.

Point number two is not the opposite of point number one. It could be slower in the action phase initially, but in three years, it could be more productive. It's all about situational leadership. There is no one best way for all situations. However, some leaders have forced this issue over the years. It is as simple as the coaching theory of fitting your players into your system or fitting your system into the players. If you could pick the exact players to fit your system, you could safely conduct the same system. However, when you don't have control of the selection of the players you must coach; it becomes tougher to fit them into your system.

It's much easier to make the system adjust to the players. They are different, with various personalities, habits and attitudes. You can't treat them all exactly the same. Adjustments will have to be made.

All urban superintendent vacancies are not the same. If an in-district candidate gets the job, chances are that the in-district person will have a different short-term plan than an outside candidate. There are jobs that demand immediate action. The house is on fire and you must put it out, NOW! However, not every district has that kind of urgency. The vision and plan must reflect the status of the district.

Visioning

Visioning is the total sum of the leader's knowledge base, experiences, hopes and dreams. Visioning is grounded in current knowledge, but it is elevated by the possibility of what could be or what should be. Urban schools are often held prisoner by the urban issues of crime, poverty, deprivation, negativism, hopelessness, and low expectations. Any vision for change and progress has to deal with changing the culture of the urban schools. The vision could involve programs, activities, curriculum, new schools, opportunities, etc. But no vision will be effectively realized without changing the school's culture.

The culture of a school or district is like the soil or dirt that allows plants to grow and flourish on earth. Without proper culture, the vision will be compromised. Therefore, the first step in formulating a vision is to ensure that the culture is right.

Culture

The school culture includes patterns of behavior, thoughts, and relationships of its people, how they speak, how they act, what they value, how they learn, how they share, and what is respected. These parts of the school or district culture form the foundation of whatever is possible in the district. Culture will determine how successful and how effective a vision will become.

Always include the needed culture foundation in your visioning. An example of a vision with culture change included is the vision this writer had for the Crispus Attucks Medical Magnet High School in Indianapolis, Indiana. I was reading a publication one day and was surprised to learn that we had very few African American born doctor candidates in our medical schools. That most doctors "of color" in our medical schools were from outside the United States of America. I talked to a doctor at the Indiana University School of Medicine and found that what I read was indeed true at Indiana University Medical School. My vision was to create a high school that started at sixth grade. Why? Because that would take students right out of elementary school before they were influenced by people telling them all the things they couldn't do. This school would be from grade six to twelve. It would be a citywide magnet school, open to students who wanted this kind of challenge. Any student could get in, but they would have to work and conduct themselves properly to stay in the school. If they were not passing and not working in the learning center after school to pass, they would be removed from the school and placed in the appropriate district boundary school. The school would have a rigorous curriculum based in Latin, math and science. Students would be able to earn high school credits in middle grades and college courses in high school. This school would have a university partner and a medical partner.

Students would be able to have medical internships by their senior year. However, they would have medical field trips and experiences throughout their schooling. The school would have a curriculum that included experiences and courses in visual arts, performing arts, and an athletic program. It would not have a football program (costs were too prohibitive). However, it would have boys' and girls' soccer teams.

Each teacher would be selected to teach in this school. The culture of the school would be based on the Four District Values of Scholarship, Excellence, Respect, and Courage; and the Ten District Culture Imperatives: (1) Children come first,; (2) All employees are accountable for student achievement that meets or exceeds state standards; (3) All employees will demonstrate professionalism and integrity; (4) Student success is the only option; (5) Potential is discovered and nurtured; (6) Academic rigor is the norm; (7) Communication is clear, open and timely; (8) Students, parents, families and community members are essential partners; (9) Diversity is valued and demonstrated by culturally competent practices; and (10) Facilities are safe, clean, secure, and inviting. All of these values and imperatives would operate in a climate of high expectations and high support.

This was my vision for Indiana's first Medical Magnet High School. In year three of operations with grades 6, 7, 8, 9, 10, and 11, the school is now a reality. The vision lives.

Planning for Implementation

This writer once wrote a book on leadership and I said, "A vision without a plan is just an hallucination." That is still very true. Many leaders have had visions, but successful leaders make their dreams come true. The plan is just as important as the vision. To transfer the vision into a plan, the vision must be effectively communicated to others. Communicating and sharing the vision with others will often enhance and improve the vision. Getting the input of others in the vision will better define and clarify the vision. Good communication is essential in this part of the process.

Once the vision has been shared, reviewed, debated, etc., it is ready to be developed into an action plan. Some would say the next step beyond the vision's definition and clarification is the feasibility stage. That is the step that looks at the reality of the vision based upon financial consider-ations, the limitation of resources, facilities, etc. But I am going beyond feasibility and possibility to the plan because one of the key elements of an effective plan is to deal with the finances, resources, etc. I want to save the "yes but" process for the review of the action plan.

The first step in creating a good plan of action is to get the right peo-ple in the planning process. These are the people with the expertise to exchange their part of the vision with concrete procedures, programs or processes. Some leaders are gifted enough to do the visioning and the planning, but most of us need the help of others to fully develop a compre-hensive action plan. In the urban setting, it is wise to get others together in a planning team to put the vision into a plan. It is recommended to have the planning team made up of staff, parents, and patrons. This allows ownership to be shared for the plan and project. It is the wise thing to do. Urban administrators, when possible, should trade time for ownership. Yes, it could be done faster inside with just staff or administrators, but it will always be the administrator's plan. If the administrator leaves, the reason for the plan leaves. This is not the best way to win friends and build support for the district. The planning team must have specific guidelines and expected outcomes. The key element of the planning process is clear and concise communications.

Once the planning committee submits its plan, the administrators have to review the plan and create an action chronology for the plan. The planning team should receive a presentation and a copy of the action plan. This keeps them in the communication circle and empowers their ownership in the plan. The action plan will define the implementation of the plan, and it should always conclude with the evaluation review of the plan's success.

The evaluation of the plan's success informs the administrators of the areas in need of improvement or change. Evaluation is always needed for continued success.

Visioning, planning, implementation, and evaluation is a very common cycle in rural, suburban and urban schools. Administrators must be sensitive to each community and situation for the best results. However, urban superintendents must demonstrate a greater urgency than most other superintendents.

Chapter 5 Case Studies

Case Study 1: Rural

You have just been selected superintendent of a small school corporation. The corporation encompasses over 150 square miles but your school membership is only 1,000 students grade p-12. When looking at past board minutes and through all your research, you see no evidence of any long- or short-range planning documents. How will you go about convincing your new board and your leadership team that a plan should be in place when they perceive no diversity and many have been in the corporation all their lives and see no reason to plan or change?

Case Study 2: Rural

A small new manufacturing plan has recently opened in your rural district. It does not employ many, but those who are employed are of a different descent than the norm for your corporation. Not only are there cultural differences, but there are language issues as well. What can you point to in a vision for a school corporation that could cover such an occurrence?

Case Study 3: Suburban

Your district has four elementary schools, two middle schools and a single 9-12 secondary school. Your scores have continued to decline, although not at an alarming pace. You have, however, begun to get more and more questions from your board on what your plan is to stop the trend. Of course, one of the issues is that your special education population has continued to grow and seems to be evenly spread out across the district. All your schools have their school improvement plans in place, but there is little consistency or communication between buildings and there is not a strategic plan (or at least a formal one) for the district. Seeing that you have only been on the job for the past two years, formulate a plan to begin to improve scores and bring continuity to the district's vision. Be sure to be as specific as possible.

Case Study 4: Urban

You have become the superintendent of a large district who has created a brand new high school. The school is currently under construction and will open next school year. This will be the third high school in this growing part of the city. They want a different, unique high school. You have been given the task of creating such a school. You have one year to create the school, employ the staff, develop the programs, and start the school year. How will you develop your vision for this school? How will you develop the plan for this unique high school? How will you ensure that this community truly feels ownership in this school? This school is in a newly annexed part of a growing urban area. How will you use knowledge from past urban progression patterns to protect the stability of this now urban high school?

Chapter 6

Time Management and the Educational Leader

Rural Perspective

Not too many years ago some construction workers were pouring concrete. When asked how tough it was to find workers to help, the owner of the company said it was sometimes difficult. He said, "I tell folks we only work half days six days a week and I can't understand why they wouldn't be happy with that." He went on to say, "Of course, when they begin the job I tell them there are 24 hours in a day." This is, of course, a bit of humor, but the district leader will have many people and organizations competing for the hours in the day and there are only 24 to give. The diverse needs of the community will be reflected in the diverse ways the superintendent must organize his/her day.

Steven Covey in his most famous work *Seven Habits of Highly Effective People* puts into perspective very well what the superintendent must do to lead effectively. In his habit of *first things first* Covey speaks of living one's life in four quadrants. These quadrants range from "important and urgent" to "not important and not urgent." Without going into too much detail, Covey lets the effective leader know that to live in the second quadrant the majority of the time would be ideal. In Covey's definition, this second quadrant is where relationships are cultivated and people are the most important aspect (Covey, 1990). This is where true leadership takes place and not management.

In a superintendent position in a rural setting, the ideal is hard to realize. Because many times there will be little if any additional central office support, the superintendent takes on many roles and assignments that would be delegated in a larger setting. As was stated before, there are only so many hours in a day, so the rural superintendent must be a highly organized individual to be able to meet the diverse needs of the position and the stakeholders that need to be served. Where larger districts would have assistant superintendents and/or directors, the rural superintendent may have to fulfill these roles as well. The management issues that would be delegated to others will fall directly on the shoulders of the already busy superintendent.

How then can the superintendent keep a balance of work, family, and personal life with all these needs coming from all directions through the community? It cannot be done without a great deal of discipline and thought. In a rural setting, the school is usually one of the larger if not the largest employer in the area. The superintendent is therefore thought of as a very important part of the community and its economic well being. Having said that, one should realize the rural superintendent may be asked and/or legally bound to serve on many committees and governmental initiatives. This takes precious time that could be used in the school setting if it were not for these responsibilities. But since the superintendent has no others to delegate the tasks to, then he/she must fulfill the responsibilities.

Having said these things, please do not think that being a rural super-intendent is not something attractive to pursue. It is a great opportunity to serve and is very rewarding when you can see the changes you can make and the lives that can be affected. A metaphor one might want to think about is that leading a rural district is like being behind the controls of a speedboat. It is quick to change directions, responsive and more easily repaired if damaged. Leading a large district, however, can be more like a luxury liner. It may have many more people, many more attractions, etc., but changing directions take much longer and the repairs are much more substantial and take much more time.

To effectively serve a rural district and the diverse needs of the students and families, the superintendent must be able to properly plan their days, weeks, months and school years to be sure they are meeting the demands of the position while keeping a life outside their office. Too many times district leaders become the position and they lose their identity and the job consumes them. Covey would say they tend to live their lives in quadrant one and three where they are consumed with the urgent and not important issues of life. Living your professional life in quadrants one and three will burn you out quickly and you will not be as effective for your stakeholders as you should be, and your family will suffer as well.

The superintendent position in a rural setting is the epitome of diversity. Not just in the ethnic sense, but in the diverse subgroups represented in every district. In a rural district the superintendent must deal with all. Examples of this are teachers, custodians, bus drivers, cooks, lawyers, board members, principals and a multitude of local civic organizations, all believing their issues are the most important in the day and the superintendent should drop everything and concentrate on them when they feel it necessary. If superintendents do not have a way to manage their time, it can get out of control easily and they can spend much more time at the office than they do away from it. Some would tell you this is "just the way it is." This author would tell you that if you are consumed by the office, then you will soon be devoured and ineffective in leading the district as it should be and deserves to be led. To be the most effective leader, you must be sure to manage your time in the most efficient manner possible.

How then can this be accomplished? Each individual has to find his/her own way of managing and prioritizing. It cannot be left to chance! Personally what this author has found to be effective is a simple "to do" list that is updated on a daily basis and is prioritized as to the time and importance of the task. As an item is crossed off, another may take its place and all others are moved up according to the need to be completed. Again, this is the first thing reviewed each morning and the last thing reviewed as one is leaving the office for the day. In this manner, the superintendent always knows what must be accomplished and in what order.

Another issue that is often overlooked in the rural superintendent position is the time set aside to think. This may sound silly, but when you are a one-person office, the day can quickly be gone and you have done nothing but manage. This is and cannot be acceptable. The superintendent must still be the educational leader of the district and must take time from the busy day to think, strategize and lead the corporation to excellence for all the diverse groups of students represented. A 30-minute block of time set aside every day to reflect and think about the needs of the district and students you lead is an absolute necessity if you are to be a successful leader of any district, and most especially a rural one.

In any district leader position it is easy to be enthralled by the position and all the responsibilities that go with it. It is especially true in a rural district because most times you will have no other administrators with whom to share the immense responsibilities at the end of the day. A precautionary note for all who wish to become or are becoming superintendents in any size, but especially the rural superintendents: You are not what you do! Put simply, a balance of who you are and what you do must be maintained. Many will want you to be superintendent 24/7 and that will burn you out and sour you on the leadership position. You must take time away to rejuvenate yourself; stays connected with your family and always keep your position in perspective. It is easy to begin to take yourself and what you do way too seriously and lose your joy. If this happens, your profession of leading and serving will suddenly become a job and not enjoyable for you or those you lead. The most important question to continue to ask yourself is, "How can I effectively lead a diverse group of students and staff if I cannot manage my diverse tasks and responsibilities in an effective manner?"

An important aspect to remember as a rural superintendent is the ability to lead versus manage. Are you recognized as a manager or a leader? According to Steven Covey, there is a difference between a manager and a leader. Managers simply maintain present conditions. For example, the rural district in which I presently serve thinks I am effective as the district superintendent if I can maintain an operational fund balance that exceeds one million dollars annually. According to Covey, this is only a factor of management; a true leader will do the same, and in addition, he/she will also find additional funding sources, provide incentives for faculty and staff to explore the resources available to improve instruction, and promote improved collaboration between parents, school and community.

Suburban Perspective

The Suburban Diverse Student Population Leader

If you were to do an Internet search on time management, you would find a myriad of articles and procedural methods on how a person can better organize and more productively utilize their daily time allotment. Methods such as Paired Comparison Analysis, Grid Analysis, the Action Priority Matrix, and the Urgent/Important Matrices are just a few examples of what the student of time management would find. The common elements in each of these and most time management strategies are prioritization, action, and urgency. For the administrator in the diverse student district, keeping those three principles of time management at the forefront of his/her daily routine is essential for maintaining success in the diverse student population district.

Prioritization

The administrator of a highly diverse school district is not unlike a clergyman who feels "called" to his profession. In a similar manner, the leader in this setting must whole-heartedly believe that the challenges of raising student achievement, preparing teachers to meet the challenges of a diverse student population, and providing the best education possible for those students is his/her most important mission. Despite the fact that peripheral requirements of the job are ever present, successful leaders in this context cannot allow themselves to lose focus of that mission. If you make sure that your daily "to do" task list contains a preponderance of items related to these areas, then the result will be the correct prioritization of your time. The key is remembering that the items that get the highest priority are the ones that get accomplished.

Action

"A sense of being overwhelmed stops action instead of encouraging it, just as a hopelessly cluttered calendar can kill urgency around a key issue. A better strategy is to identify three or four ideas that will be easy to implement, and start doing so immediately....Remember, words are not the test. Action is the test. Never forget furious activity and running and meeting and slick presentations are not a sign of true urgency." (Kotter, 2008).

This quote from Kotter is a reminder of the necessity to keep the main agenda of the daily workload limited to that which is most critical to the mission of the district. If the focus of the administrator in pursuing the vision of improved achievements for all students is to be accomplished, then they must keep the daily actions to three or four ideas. In addition, these few, but focused, agenda items should be reachable goals that are measurable. If there is no measurable evidence of these actions showing progress toward the intended mission of raising student achievement, preparing teachers to meet the challenges of a diverse student population, and providing the best education available for this population, then those actions are wasted.

Urgency

In Kotter's book, *A Sense of Urgency*, the author delineates between "false" urgency and "true" urgency. For the administrator managing his/her time in the context of a diverse student population, it is important to note the differences between the two so that the successful leader is able to avoid a hurried and unimportant agenda. The author suggests that true urgency is "measurably important" in a changing world context, that it seems equally important to all persons in the organization, and that it creates a powerful desire to move forward and "to win, now." Finally, he suggests that true urgency is "alert, fast moving, and focused on important issues," while it "purges irrelevant activities" (Kotter, 2008). In the daily agenda of the school administrator in a diverse school community, these descriptors should be the ruling guideposts that determine true urgency each day.

Urban Perspective

Time cannot be borrowed, stored, or recycled; it can only be spent as it is received, twenty-four hours in each day. Thus, time management means self management, managing oneself with respect to a non controllable resource.

—Dr. Ivan Fitzwater

Urban school administrators have just their eight to twelve plus hours per day. To be an effective urban administrator, you are forced to focus on people during the school day, and paper plus all the rest after the people go home for the day. This is not how it was supposed to be, but it is the common reality of administrative supervision of operations, instruction, student behavior, student activities, meetings, etc. Time passes rapidly during the average school day, but there are a few practices that could allow administrators to better organize their limited time.

The Daily Routine

Each day is unpredictable, but urban administrators have seen enough of them to know that there is a common pattern to the abnormal school day. This common pattern allows administrators to organize their days into some daily routine. The daily routine consists of four primary blocks of time.

There is the early morning block of time from 7:00 a.m. or earlier to 10:00 a.m. There is the mid morning block from 10:00 a.m. to 12:30 p.m. There is the afternoon block from 12:30 p.m. to 4:00 p.m. and there is the early evening block of time from 4:00 p.m. to 8:00 p.m.

Early Morning Block Pre 7:00 a.m. to 10:00 a.m.	Mid Morning Block 10:00 a.m. to 12:30 p.m.
Afternoon Break 12:30 p.m. to 4:00 p.m.	Early Evening Block 4:00 p.m. to 8:00 p.m.

Beyond 8:00 p.m. you work at your own risk. The risks are a loss of personal time, a loss of family time, a loss of entertainment, a loss of vocational balance, and a loss of recovery time. A few nights per month are guaranteed to take some of this beyond 8:00 p.m. time, but every night or every school night could create serious personal, family and professional concerns. It should be clearly understood, an urban school administrator cannot worry about putting time into the job. The job demands time, but how we manage that time is the key.

The Early Morning Block ~ 7:00 a.m. – 10:00 a.m.

School administrators often get to school an hour before school starts, or earlier, for the day. This is a great time to plan and review the known activities for the day. It is strongly recommended that administrators keep a daily log of planned activities. The time before school starts is a good opportunity to review the day's activities.

The log activities could be assigned to the four time blocks. It is a good practice to schedule most planned meetings between 9:00 a.m. and noon or after 4:00 p.m. A half hour before the start of school should find administrators out and about the building. Some will have assigned areas to cover and others may move about freely. Make every effort to avoid being in meetings during the period of 30 minutes before classes start and 30 minutes after the start of classes. It is important for administrators to see students in the mornings. They get to know the students and the students know where to find them.

The early morning block provides ideal opportunities for classroom observations and walk-throughs, loose ends or unfinished business from the last school day to be addressed.

Another important reason to be out and about early in the mornings is to meet and greet teachers. It is great to show them how much you appreciate what they do for the students. You also tend to catch those teachers who are running late or cutting it too close. They need to know that you know and, if needed, they will have to answer for their tardiness.

The Early Morning Block allows administrators to really maximize their presence and start each day on a sound note. It forces administrators to organize activities and meetings at the most appropriate time of the early morning.

The Mid Morning Block ~ 10:00 a.m. to 12:30 p.m.

The Mid Morning Block is an essential block for administrators. In schools, this block will often include lunch time for students and possible lunch for the administrator. This is another good time for classroom observations and walk-throughs. Parent meetings could be scheduled in this block as well as other meetings. Administrators should never "hang out" or waste this time block. There is always something to do during the Mid Morning Block of time. Never waste a mid morning.

The Afternoon Block ~ 12:30 p.m. to 4:00 p.m.

The Afternoon Block of time is very important because it could save you from doing some of those things after 4:00 p.m. Classroom observation, walk-throughs, meetings, and some paperwork could be completed in this important block of time. Don't put off things for tomorrow if they can be done this afternoon. Complete your "to do" list and prepare to see the students off at the end of the school day. As is the practice before the start of the school day, it is a good routine to be out on the halls at least 15 minutes before students are dismissed for the day. Students need to know that you are around just in case they have something that can't wait until tomorrow to share with you. Getting out to see students off each day will not be an easy thing to do, but you must schedule it and get it done.

After students leave there are people to see ... teachers, administrators, support staff. Sometimes there are meetings to conduct or attend. This is often a busy part of the day.

The Early Evening Block ~ 4:00 p.m. to 8:00 p.m.

This is the danger zone of the day. It is often quiet and it is a great time to just "think." It is also time to finish the e-mails, paperwork and make those phone calls. Often, it could be time to supervise an after-school ball game, dance, club activity, etc. It is very important to structure this time and try to complete your tasks as soon as possible. Some days will be late days, but you can't allow all of them to be late. You are the master or the slave to this time of day. So much will depend on how well you take care of this time. A study by Joseph Trickett of successful and unsuccessful executives indicates that a characteristic of failing executives is their readiness to sacrifice their family lives to their occupational lives. In general, a neglect of the family and an overemphasis on the job at the expense of the marriage will eventually lower job performance (Trickett, 1962).

Time Wasters

The Four Time Blocks are good organizational tools, but time-saving practices are even more important for time management. The answer to saving time is within each of us. The problem with wasting time is within each of us. We are the answer to the problem. There are practices we must change or add to help us deal more effectively with time utilization.

Many of the following time wasters were taken from R. Alec MacKenzie's 1972 List. They are still relevant today.

- People who often lack time to get things done are often their own greatest enemy. The heart of the time management problem is the management of self.

- Inability to start or end meetings on time.

- Frequently caught up in routine tasks that others could do.

- Lack of priorities.

- Too much personal attention to issues.

- Poor communication.

- Common mistakes.

- Attempting to do too much too soon or all at once.

- Procrastinating.

- Lack of organization.

- Failure to listen.

- Inability to say no.

- No one can do the job like I can.

- Failure to delegate to others.

- Delegating responsibility without authority.

- Blaming others.

- Too many personal and outside activities.

- Bypassing the chain of command.

Peter Drucker once said, "Unless he manages himself effectively, no amount of ability, skill, experience, or knowledge will make an executive effective." Time wasters are created and eliminated by one person. I would guess more than 95 percent of time wasters are created by the person wasting the time.

Leadership Styles and Time Management

Some urban superintendents are constantly putting out fires and dealing with "action now!" situations. These situations can destroy planned "to do" list procedures. However, the smart urban superintendent will learn to classify situations, some of which may be urgent, into patterns of controlled actions. No matter how urgent the problem or how important the issue, there is still just one superintendent to deal with it. So, the style of the leader becomes very important in dealing with problems and situations and controlling the use of time.

Robert F. Pearse conducted a study on "The Effects of an Executive's Leadership Style on His Time Management Practices" in the early 1970s. He studied the effect of individual leadership styles on executive skills such as planning, delegating, and decision making.[1] He developed the following typical style-related time use patterns:

1. Task and Achievement Orientation – The executive with a strong need to finish tasks personally typically has difficulty delegating. The inner compulsion to finish things makes him feel worthy doing so. Combined with the role of the hard, intense worker, it leads him to pour large amounts of time and energy into doing rather than managing.

2. Leadership, Dominance, and Decision Orientation – Executives with strong impulses to play the hard-hitting leader role enjoy dominating and controlling subordinates and pride themselves on quick decision making. There is a "take charge" role, and they have difficulty delegating.

3. Impulsive and Physically Energetic Orientation – These are fast-moving, energetic, action-oriented men who see the executive's job as that of a "shaker and mover." They are often frantically active, making impulsive decisions and moving back and forth from office to plant with high physical energy.

4. Socially Warm, Colorful, and Personal Orientation – Executives who are high in a need to be noticed enjoy social interaction, like to be emotionally close in interpersonal styles, and tend to spend much of their time in interpersonal relations. Their style contrasts with the task- and achievement-oriented type. They are very successful in positions requiring political relationships, close customer contacts, and the like.

5. Theoretical, Detail, and Structure Orientation – The theoretical-minded executive is apt to spend much time in care-

ful analysis of abstractions and concepts. He is important in technological companies. He may overlook the practical or implementation part of his work. With a high need to attend to detail personally, he may become a nit picker if not careful. He slows things down by his preoccupation with detail and tends to spend time setting up systems and rigid organization patterns in which he feels more comfortable. He may have emotional difficulty moving freely in unstructured situations.

6. Change, New-Experience, and Feeling-Expression Orientation – The change- oriented executive becomes bored with routine. He seeks new experiences and resents work that requires time used in a repetitive pattern. The emotionally calm executive tends to use time in ways that will insulate him from emergencies.

7. Followership Orientation and Defensive-Aggressive Orientation – The executive who needs to defer to authority spends much time in seeking to please the boss. He is often regarded as "trustworthy."If he does not carry his followership to excess, he may be emotionally soothing to supervisors, but he has difficulty managing his own time on independent assignments where he is unable to check with his boss for assurance he is doing what most pleases him. The rules- and supervision-oriented executive has difficulty structuring his own time unless he has carefully spelled out rules and regulations to go by. He is most comfortable in bureaucratic organizations where he may carry out assignments by the book. The defensive-aggressive executive carries a large chip on his shoulder and spends time arguing with others. He may feel others are out to get

him. He loves a good fight and so attacks or counterattacks either in one-to-one business relationships or on teams or committees.

Pearse recommends that executives be trained in the skill of time utilization to improve their ability to handle paperwork, delegation, supervision, and planning. Urban superintendents should be knowledgeable of Robert F. Pearse's study because it will allow them to better understand personal administrative styles, practices and possible outcomes. It should also allow them to better understand their personal styles and how to improve the effectiveness of their performance.

Time Records

Time is too valuable to be taken for granted. The urban superintendent has to organize time as efficiently as possible because it is so limited. For urban superintendents, there is only today and short time ahead. How each day is planned is important and there are really very few long-term projects. From this writer's experiences, projects and activities should be planned in a month to a two-year maximum time line. Sure, there will be some longer term facility planning and some real property considerations, but most of the urban agenda is now or very soon.

To plan for the maximum use of each day, a plan calendar with meetings, activities, and special events must be maintained. Current technology enables us to use Blackberry phones and other devices to plan. However, there is still no better system than a reliable secretary or administrative assistant. All meetings should be planned and/or scheduled ahead, if possible. Try to avoid scheduling a meeting on the day of the meeting. A few other tips to consider:

- If possible, allow your secretary or assistant to keep your calendar and to schedule your meetings. This will enable your assistant to follow the rules you outline for setting appointments and meetings. It will be one less thing to worry about and it will create better balance for your day.

- If you don't know where your time is disappearing to each day, keep a 30- to 60-day time log. After the designated time log period, analyze your time. How long or what is the average time spent meeting with one individual? What is your average time for group meetings? How much time is taken for lunch? What are the common interruptions and how long do they last? Who interrupts you the most and why? How much time is spent on e-mail? How much time on the telephone? These are just a few questions to answer and find ways to improve, if needed. These time logs can be simple or comprehensive. It just depends on how much you need to know. There are also time surveys, inventories, and profiles to ascertain how much time is used.

Last Word on Time

There are many books, papers, studies and ideas about how to maximize the use of time. However, after all the research is completed, the use of time is a personal decision. Dr. Benjamin E. Mays, former President of Morehouse College, said it best:

> "I have only just a minute
> Only sixty seconds in it,
> Forced upon me – can't refuse it,

Didn't seek it, didn't choose it.
But it's up to me to use it.
I must suffer if I lose it.
Give account if I abuse it,
Just a tiny little minute –
But eternity is in it."

Time management is a personal responsibility. For the urban super-intendent, it is a valuable commodity. It must be defended and its use planned effectively. Time is enhanced through sound administrative practices of solid scheduling, eliminating time wasters, reducing interruptions, delegating responsibilities to others, forward planning, setting priorities and doing first things first, training your secretary or assistant to help you maximize your time, handling communication efficiently, training your administrators to use time more effectively and always making time a priority. You are in charge of running an urban school district and it all runs on time. Manage yourself and master your time.

Chapter 6 Case Studies

Case Study 1: Rural

You have the following list of things that must be addressed today. How will you prioritize and why? Complete a simple "to do" list with highest priority first to least important. Be prepared to defend your decisions.

a.   Board president calls and wants to meet with you ASAP.

b.   You have a progress meeting on new construction at 9:00 a.m.

c.   You are speaking at Rotary at lunch.

d.   The union president calls and wants to present you with a grievance.

e.   An attorney from the ACLU calls and demands you remove the Ten Commandments from your office wall.

f.   You have a regular scheduled board meeting tonight.

g.   There is an approaching snow storm that should begin to hit around 1:00 p.m.

h.   Your granddaughter has a solo in her school's musical tonight.

Case Study 2: Suburban

Your situation as a new superintendent of this suburban school system is that the former leader has been severely criticized for not being visible in the buildings and in the community. With all you have to do in your new position, you can understand how difficult it is to be "out and about" within your district. When they interviewed you, the board let you know this was very important to them and your stakeholders. How will you manage your time so that you can be in your buildings and in the community organizations that want you to participate? Be sure to be specific on how you would go about managing your time effectively and stating how you will measure your success.

Case Study 3: Urban

You are the superintendent of an urban school district and your executive administrative assistant was killed last week in a tragic automobile accident. Now you must find a new executive administrative assistant and train her to schedule, protect your time calendar, and run your office. What are the qualities you are seeking in this person? All things being equal with the candidates, what will be the overall deciding factor for selection?

After you have selected the new assistant, how will you train her to take care and control of your time?

Chapter 7

Crisis Management

Rural Perspective

A rural superintendent received a panic phone call from his new elementary principal who had come to the small community via a nearby college town. When the principal got the district leader to the phone, she began to relay the terrible incident she needed help with to decide what to do. It seems a fifth grade boy had driven a tractor to school and the principal was beside herself and needed help in deciding how to discipline the boy. The superintendent asked where the tractor was, and the principal replied, in the field across the street. The superintendent asked if the student had driven the tractor on school grounds and she replied no. The superintendent then asked why she was upset. The fact was the student had just done what his farmer father had directed him to do. He drove the tractor (a dual rear wheel John Deere) to school because he was to work the field as soon as he got out of school. The principal was directed to leave the boy alone and let him go to work as soon as school was over. What is one school's crisis is another school's normal daily activity.

Each community is diverse in its needs, as is the student population is diverse. When looking at the school crisis management plan, the district leader must be aware of what normal daily activity for their district is, and what are normal cultural activities for the community and the children attending school in the district.

There are some things, however, that will be the same no matter what size or where the district is located. The tragedy in Columbine was a wake-up to all school systems across the country, no matter how large or small, of how a wonderful school can be devastated by the random acts of violence of an individual or individuals. The days of not taking threats seriously are gone forever, and now each threat must be handled as a real concern for the students for which we are responsible.

When designing a crisis management team and plan, the diverse needs of the student body must be considered. All faith groups and cultures should have representatives on the team so the children they serve can be assisted in times of need. Most states now mandate such a plan and team but they do not set forth the make-up of the members or their training. It is imperative that careful consideration be given to all groups represented in the school community when putting together the team and the plan. A checklist of the different faith-based groups might be helpful as well as the ethnicity represented within the school. The reason for this diverse group of individuals is so each student can have the support they need when a crisis occurs.

All prospective district leaders must realize that it is not *if* a crisis will happen on their watch, it is *when* it will happen. To not be prepared is unacceptable and could be career- ending if not handled in the proper manner. In times of crisis, the district leader must be the calming influence in the school community and must be ready to lead the school through the traumatic events.

The kinds of things that can and probably will happen are student and/ or staff suicides, natural disasters, weather-related disasters, bomb threats, personal threats on staff and/or students, building issues (water, sewage, heat, cooling, electrical, etc.) that cause a disruption in the educational day. All of these take a cool head and a firm plan on how to deal with the crisis to be sure all stakeholders are kept safe and education is back on schedule as quickly as possible.

Even in a rural district the head of the crisis team may not be the superintendent. The person could be one of the building principals or a teacher, or support staff person who has been properly trained in crisis management and has been involved from the inception of the crisis management plan. The make-up of the team will vary from school to school, but here are some suggestions for the team composition:

1. Members of local law enforcement agencies

2. Counselors

3. Members of local clergy

4. Member of local fire department

5. School administrators

6. At least one physician

7. A board member

8. A bus driver

9. The head maintenance person

One of the main keys in this group and the plan itself is to attempt to identify as many possible situations where the team may be needed. The plan should be as detailed as possible and must be update at least each semester as some of the people on the team may leave or be replaced by other representatives. A call chain should be established and a central meeting place should be identified.

As a leader who has gone through this process and made some serious mistakes as well as doing some things right, let me tell you that the more detailed the plan and the more rigorous the training and education of the staff and the crisis team, the better it will function in the times it is needed. Of all the things done wrong, the lack of appropriate training was the biggest issue that was not completed in a professional manner. It is a necessity that all team members be well trained, especially the clergy who will be serving.

We failed to properly train one of our clergy members and when we had a sixth grade student commit suicide, our team was called into action and did an admirable job in handling the situation, with the exception of the one clergy member. Instead of consoling and helping a child through the trauma of the loss of a friend, the minister took the opportunity to try to convert the child rather than help them through a time of crisis. In a public school setting not only is this not appropriate, but it is illegal as well, and the minister, although well meaning, put the entire team and the corporation at risk because he had not been trained adequately as to what his role was and specifically what he was to do.

Each school staff must also be trained and educated as to their role in crisis management and what they can and cannot do in these times. A standard lock-down process with appropriate codes should be adopted and periodic dry runs should be conducted so students and staff as well as parents are aware of the standard operating procedures during a time of crisis.

There will, of course, be other kinds of crises that as the school's leader you will have to handle. There will be the teacher involved with the student, the teachers involved with the teachers, and the list goes on. The key to handling any crisis situation is to always be prepared, think, and follow your standard policy and procedures. Many school leaders forget their school law classes when they take the leader chair and forget their legal safeguards that are available to them if they follow the district policies. When they go outside those policies is when the crisis can be career threatening. If one stays inside the board-adopted policies, they have immunity; if they go outside them, they forego said immunity.

In any crisis situation the leader must realize the Latin term "in loco parentis" and treat each child under their care as if they were there own. The term means "in place of the parent" and when children are in school, no matter what diverse group they come from, the school leader must treat them as they would their own child and keep them safe at all costs.

The rural superintendent must recognize the relationship between diversity and response to crisis. For example, African Americans may not view a present crisis situation as such. There is research to support the fact that one person's thoughts on adversity may not be viewed the same way within all cultures. Culture plays an important role in how African Americans view adversity and crisis because of their history of such. The resilience and effective coping strategies displayed by African Americans is linked to their cultural beliefs, behaviors, and practices that produce positive outcomes during adversity.

Suburban Perspective

When Crisis Comes – Attitude

Leaders in a crisis situation can either make or break the crisis by their initial response to it. Jonathan Bernstein, a consultant and expert on crisis management, suggests that "attitude is everything" in a crisis situation. In his article "The Three C's of Credibility in Crisis," he cites research from a UCLA study that indicates up to 93 percent of communication effectiveness is determined by non-verbal cues. He says that to be seen as a credible leader in a crisis situation, the spokesperson (usually the administrator in a school setting) needs to be compassionate, and to appear competent and confident. The administrator in any district (with a diverse student population or not) should keep these three concepts in mind in a crisis. No matter what the crisis, by displaying compassion, competence, and confidence in a difficult situation, you will reduce fear and anxiety among teachers, fellow administrators, and students, as well as the media.

The Uniqueness of the Diverse Population Crisis

The nature of a crisis in a non-homogeneous, diverse school district can have some unique social or legal implications. One social issue that the school leader may have to address in a crisis situation is the question of race and possible implications that appear to be discriminatory. When the crisis has such an implied issue inherent in it, the response for the administrator must be to negate (regardless of the crisis) the chance for such assumptions to do harm to students and to potentially initiate unrest in the school community. In addition, the administrator must be knowledgeable in students' rights and, specifically, be familiar with the Federal Education Rights and Privacy Act and the legal implications of it in a crisis situation. If an administrator violates a student's rights under this law in a highly publicized crisis situation, he or she will very likely put the district, as well as themselves, in a highly litigious situation. To prevent this, the school leader must know what kind of information is appropriate to share and what is not allowed under the law. Sometimes telling "all" to the wrong audience can initiate a firestorm of response. The wise administrator only shares pertinent and legal information in a crisis situation.

Finally, the administrator must keep in mind at all times and in all crisis situations that students' welfare must be his or her main objective throughout. The possible impact of a crisis can have a psychological impact on the student or students directly involved in the crisis as well as on students directly removed from it. How you respond can and will dictate the degree of trauma felt at the student level.

Lessons Learned – Three Examples of Crisis

The recent demographic shifts in the number of Latinos increasing in numbers in United States cities across the country who are primarily from Mexico and Central America have caused a series of recent school-related crises. This occurred when the ICE (Immigration and Customs Enforcement) conducted raids in communities where they suspected that a high number of the Latino population were undocumented citizens. These raids directly and immediately impacted their children because a majority of these children were enrolled in public schools. Case law has determined that public schools cannot deny individual rights (in this case, an education) to a child on the basis of their undocumented citizen status. The crisis, which made national news, in each case, came about when the ICE raided local businesses and factories in three U.S cities and arrested the parents of many Latino students. This took place in Greeley, Colorado;

Grand Island, Nebraska; and New Bedford, Massachusetts. These raids resulted in chaos and fear among the Latino population as most of these parents on the day of the raid had no chance, prior to being arrested, to make arrangements for the long-term care of their children, the majority of whom were in school at the time of the raids. The Urban Institute in 2007 sponsored a case study report entitled, "Paying the Price: The Impact of Immigration Raids on America's Children." In the study, there were a number of lessons learned that all administrators in diverse schools communities should heed in a crisis situation. For instance, the Grand Island, Nebraska, schools in preparation for such a raid had a contact database that included detailed information about the parents' employers. This allowed them to contact all of the parents at the raided sites. In addition, on the day of the raid, teachers and staff conducted one-on-one interviews with children of parents arrested to ensure that each child had a caretaker to contact in the case that they were left alone. The bus drivers taking students home on the day of the raid were instructed to not drop students where there was no parent or trusted adult to greet them. Finally, the school district directed all staff and teachers to maintain calm and to reassure the safety of not only the students affected, but to also assure those students that their parents were safe.

These few examples of real response to crisis are important for school administrators to note, but more importantly, the long-term impact of the trauma these events caused on this subgroup of students and their parents needs to be addressed. Making sure that the schools are a safe haven for students (even in the threat of a federal agency) is a principle of which we must never lose sight.

The study provided three recommendations for public schools in such a crisis. The first was that school districts should develop a systemwide plan that ensures children have a safe place to go in such an emergency and that they reduce the risk of children being left without adult supervision. Second, the school district should make sure that counseling and academic support be provided for these affected children for an extended time. The third recommendation is that schools, churches, and other community entities that could help in this situation should have community forums to discuss the aftermath of these actions to reduce fear and tension in the community. In short, the best plan for a crisis is to plan before it happens.

Urban Perspective

The urban superintendent should understand that a superintendent can be a manager without being a leader; however a superintendent cannot be a great leader without being a manager. Management is a chief part of leadership. The leader's skills of creating the vision, the plan, the strategies and implementation do not progress to a productive outcome unless the leader or his designees effectively deal with the management issues of making it work. Leaders work today in tomorrow's domain, but managers work for the success and the good of today. The superintendent creates the vision, plan, strategies and activities to start a Medical Magnet High School, but his management skills will determine the success or effectiveness of the school. Crisis management is truly crisis in operations. Urban superintendents must have the management skills and know how to resolve and correct critical problems in operations. This is truly a requirement for survival in the job.

Crisis Identification

"The schools of the urban crisis, as they now exist, perpetuate the cycle of poverty, the merry-go-round of despair and frustration. They consciously or inadvertently discriminate against the poor and the powerless." These words and quotations are taken from the 1969 "Task Force on Urban Education, Schools of Urban Crisis." Urban superintendents should know that historically urban school districts have been in crisis. The foundational roots of the crisis have been poverty, despair, frustration, crime, hopelessness, racial, and socio-economic discrimination. These root issues exacerbate the other routine crisis topics of finance, union issues, teacher quality, teacher shortages, administrative preparation, and other operational issues. To lead an urban school district, the superintendent must deal with crisis as an expected norm. As Peter F. Drucker said, "The symptom to look for is the recurrent 'crisis,' the crisis that comes back year after year. A crisis that recurs a second time is a crisis that must not occur again."

The urban superintendent must learn the symptoms and signs of approaching crisis and develop appropriate strategies to resolve them as proactively as possible. The same crisis should not occur annually. It has to be corrected and prevented or avoided the next time. Drucker said, "…prevent or reduced (a crisis) to a routine which clerks can manage. The definition of a 'routine' is that it makes unskilled people without judgment capable of doing what it took near-genius to do before; for a routine put down in systematic, step-by-step form what a very able man learned in surmounting yesterday's crisis." All of this is based on the identification of the problem or crisis. Developing the proper definition of the problem is the first step toward the answer for the crisis. Prior to the appointment of Robert McNamara as the Secretary of Defense for the United States of America, the government had a last-minute crisis each fourth quarter of the budget year. This crisis shook the entire American defense establishment every spring, toward the end of the fiscal year on June 30. Every manager in the defense establishment, military or civilian, tried desperately in May and June to find expenditures for the money appropriated by Congress for the fiscal year. Otherwise, McNamara was afraid he would have to give back the money. He immediately saw that this crisis was unnecessary because the law had always permitted the placing of unspent dollars that were needed, into an interim account. This "so-called" crisis was created because they failed to research and understand the spending regulations. But it had been a crisis for years. A very similar "crisis" was occurring in an urban school district every October and November because unspent

Title dollars had to be spent or they would be returned to the state. The district purchased many unneeded, poorly considered items and also lost hundreds of thousands of dollars because of a faulty budgetary routine and inadequate planning for excess funds. This was not a crisis once the problem was clearly defined.

When is the issue or concern a crisis? Who defines the crisis? It is strongly recommended that nothing is declared a crisis until the superintendent names it a crisis. One patron's or parent's crisis might be solved easily by the appropriate person. Superintendents must protect themselves from alarmist people who often run about the place crying, "The sky is falling!" The sky is not falling until the matter is examined, defined, and named by the superintendent. This becomes very important when communicating with the media and the public.

Crisis: Managing Communication

Urban superintendents are very accustomed to the media in all of its forms. Video, print, blogs, and other forms of mass communication are common and often daily occurrences. However, communications in any form should never be taken for granted. If there is a crisis in the district, it has to be communicated to the appropriate persons in the most timely, respectful and professional manner.

Communication Protocol

The urban superintendent must have formal communication procedures, guidelines and steps in place to deal with crisis situations.

1. All information should be directed to the designated administrator or the superintendent.

2. No statements will be given by any district employee except the person designated by the superintendent. This person is commonly the district's public relations person, a designated administrator or the superintendent.

3. There will be one central point for the distribution of the information to the staff, media and public. This communication will be presented via press conference, staff meeting, live media, and telephone messaging system to parents and community leaders, news releases, letters and follow-up meetings.

4. The message must be jargon free; clearly spoken or written; brief, but comprehensive; and indicate if there will be additional information forthcoming.

5. If possible, try to create some "commonly asked questions" and answer them. If a press conference is held, leave time for questions after the presentation.

6. Remember to be truthful and as brief as possible. Don't over-tell the story.

The urban school setting can produce many possible crisis situations. The most important approach for an urban superintendent is to have solid communication with staff, parents, students, and the community. Be proactive and communicate. If one of the schools is experiencing gang problems, don't hide it from the staff, students, and parents. Communicate the concern and the actions you will take to deal with the problem. Update them on how the situation is progressing. Never attempt to hide this kind of problem because it could explode suddenly and put others in danger. It is not a negative reflection on the school to have a gang problem. But to allow it to exist and not share the concern with others is a major problem.

Crisis: Leadership

Urban school districts are tough to lead in the best of times and situations. However, in crisis, leadership is the key to overcoming the situation. Having the right superintendent in place is very important for urban districts. What are the leadership qualities needed to deal with the crisis issues of the urban school districts? Abraham Lincoln was the president who really came to understand the crisis of leadership. The Confederate States of America seceded from the Union taking all federal agencies, forts, and arsenals within their territory only ten days before he took office. He was only elected by a minority of the popular vote and many had a very low opinion of him and viewed him as a second-rate country lawyer. He had little or no leadership experience, but he had some very special qualities that enabled him to become a great leader.

Horace Greeley once said of Lincoln's excellence, "He was not a born king of men...but a child of the common people, who made himself a great persuader, therefore a leader, by dint of firm resolve, patient effort, and dogged perseverance. He slowly won his way to eminence and fame by doing the work that lay next to him—doing it with all his growing might—doing it as well as he could, and learning by his failure, when failure was encountered, how to do it better... He was open to all impressions and influences, and gladly profiled by the teaching of events and circumstances, no matter how adverse or unwelcome. There was probably no year of his life when he was not a wiser, cooler, and better man than he had been the year preceding."

Now there aren't too many Abraham Lincolns around, but his leadership practices are sound and are used by many leaders. Lincoln was very sure of himself and he had a natural ability to persuade others. He transformed the office of the presidency during the Civil War through his leadership. He believed in assertive leadership or "taking the bull by the horns." Lincoln learned on the job and earned the respect and trust of his followers. He delegated and coached instead of dictating. He was completely involved in the war effort and learned how to be the commander-in-chief. He studied and mastered military strategies and tactics. He mastered the general organization of the government and how to effectively work in it.

Like Jim Collins' "Good to Great" view, Lincoln believed that you need to get the right person before you deal with the "what." Lincoln looked for his "Grant" and Collins needed the right person to deal with the right people on the bus. Urban superintendents know that people are the answer. The right people will ensure success, but the wrong people will defeat the effort.

Lincoln also knew you couldn't deal with problems unless you got out to see what was happening in the field. Urban superintendents must get out and see what is happening and talk with the people. Lincoln believed in building strong alliances and urban superintendents truly understand how important it is to build relationships and sound communications both formally and informally before the crisis.

Lincoln believed in exercising a strong hand when needed. He was honest and decisive. Circumstances or crises motivated Lincoln to be innovative and creative. To do this, he had to study and find new interpretations of the Constitution and other legal documents. This even included his oath of office as president. Some people criticized him for excessive power, called him a tyrant or dictator, but he understood his power and knew what he had to do. Urban superintendents must be creative and innovative to deal with the various problems and crises of leadership. They must borrow Lincoln's attitude of research and study. They must know the limits of their power and authority. They must seek better ways, new ways to find solutions to problems and concerns.

Lincoln also had a great quality of listening to people. He was open-minded and flexible about ideas and decisions. He didn't play games with people and if he disagreed with them, he would let them know. Lincoln would focus, and direct his people to do the appropriate things, but he very seldom dictated to them. He influenced, hinted or made suggestions for action. Urban superintendents must learn to listen and really attempt to hear what others are saying. They need to be open-minded and flexible. Urban superintendents need to support the efforts of their followers. When they come up with good ideas, let them go ahead and try them. Monitor their progress. If they succeed, give them credit, and if they fail, take the blame and help them to improve. These are solid practices from the times of Lincoln. They are still very relevant today.

Crisis and Opportunities

In the urban school districts of this country, there are common operational crises. Crisis motivates urban superintendents to improve operations and to find innovative and creative ways to solve problems and concerns.

Effective urban superintendents use crisis situations as opportunities to get various things done. All crises create concerns and problems, but they don't have to be all bad. There are ways to utilize crises to get things done.

It is major crises to have a first grade student not show up at home after school, for example. He was on the bus after school, but he didn't get home. The bus driver said he checked the bus and no one was left. So he took the bus to the bus shelter. However, after a major search of the community, the young man wasn't found. Security went to the bus shelter and rechecked the bus and found the young man asleep on the back of the bus. The driver insisted he checked the bus, but he was dismissed from his job for failing to do his job and gross negligence. After the bad public feedback and negative commentary, the superintendent changed the procedure for bus drivers in how they checked their buses. They even installed a special alarm on the back of each bus that forced each driver to walk to the back of the bus to disengage the buzzer before the bus's ignition could be turned off. All of this, plus an automatic loss of employment by the bus driver, goes a long way in preventing this crisis from happening again.

In another example, poor supervision at the high school homecoming dance allowed some intoxicated students to attend the affair and create a major disturbance. This led to a fight among the students and it all ended up on the late night and early morning news. This created a major negative mark against the school. From this situation, the superintendent and principal used the negative to change the procedure for attendance at all school dances. Now breathalyzer tests must be taken by each student before they may enter any school dance or party. Unless the major problem at the homecoming dance had occurred, it would not have been very popular to initiate this kind of check and supervision.

In a third example, a common personnel crisis for urban school districts is having teaching shortages in the math, science, and special education courses. Teacher universities and pre-service teacher programs fail to produce enough candidates willing to teach in the urban setting. This creates a crisis in these teaching areas annually for many urban school districts. This provides the opportunity for creative urban superintendents to work with transition to teaching programs to produce candidates in the shortage areas of math, science and special education. It also creates the opportunity to work with unique teacher programs like "Teach for America" or "The New Teacher Project."

Again, crisis events are major problems, but they can provide great opportunities for innovative and creative urban superintendents.

Chapter 7 Case Studies

Case Study 1: Rural

Your elementary principal calls to inform you that there has been a bank robbery at a bank located near your lone elementary. The police have informed the principal that the robber is on the loose and still in the area of the bank and school. Your principal has called a code "yellow" which means all outside doors are locked with no one to go in and out, and the inside of the building is continuing with school as usual. The problem is the principal has some parents who have heard what is going on and are at the door demanding their children. What do you tell your principal to do, and why?

Case Study 2: Suburban

It has been the wettest April in recent history. You have some buildings under renovation projects and although they are under roof, there are still areas that are not nearly completed. On a Sunday night you have another severe storm and the already saturated ground cannot take any more water. Your high school building begins to take on water and several of the roads in your district have running water going across them. It is 10 p.m. on Sunday night and you receive two calls—one from your transportation director informing you of the road closures, and the second from your board president wanting to know what you are going to do. Explain your decision-making process and how you would use the resources at your disposal.

Case Study 3: Urban

You are the superintendent of a large urban school district in the eastern part of the United States. Your high school principals called to tell you that they had a union meeting and decided that administrators will only work the school day and will not cover any after-school events or activities because they are upset and unhappy with the lack of progress in their negotiation with the district negotiator. You know that this is basketball, wrestling, gymnastics, and holiday season and each evening is loaded with district school activities. The administrative union contract forbids strikes or work slow-downs, but it really doesn't speak to after-school activities or a formal workday for administrators. You understand how important it is to have administrators at special events and sports activities. What will you do to deal with the situation? Will you cancel the after-school activities and sports contests? How will you communicate this crisis to others?

Chapter 8

Curriculum Assessment and Development

Rural Perspective

Curriculum development and assessment is one of the most important parts of any district's success in meeting the diverse needs of the student population. This author also believes it is even more important in the rural setting to be sure the curriculum is assessed as it relates to diversity, because in many rural districts the only chance for children to be introduced into cultures other than their own is through the school's curricular process. While the curriculum must be aligned with state and national standards, it can be done so and still introduce students to cultures and mores that they might not otherwise be exposed to.

There are several issues that can cause the rural leader problems when dealing with curricular alignment and assessment. District leaders must, however, realize that one of the most important roles they have in their plethora of responsibilities in a rural leadership position is that of instructional leader and proponent of a rigorous and aligned curriculum. Just because a school is small in size does not mean the curriculum should not be aligned vertically and horizontally and also that it must be rigorous and meet and exceed the minimum standards. Superintendent must take the lead in research and development and use what limited resources at their disposal to be sure the curriculum is up to date and adequate to meet the needs of the students.

There are many obstacles that must be overcome in the rural curricular development area. Some of those are:

1. Limited number of teachers at grade level and subject area

2. Past neglect of curricular initiatives

3. Limited number of course offerings at the secondary level

4. Limited amount of people to champion curricular design

5. Inconsistency in staffing

6. Lack of board interest

Let us examine each of these potential roadblocks and see how the rural district leader can overcome the obstacle.

Limited Teachers at Grade and Subject Level

Superintendent cannot create more jobs when they have no more students, so to solve this problem is not easy. What must happen is that leaders must use all resources possible to allow those limited number of staff to optimize their time and expertise to align and map the curriculum. Back to the earlier metaphor used with the speedboat, this lack of people can be viewed as a positive versus a negative, and the curriculum mapping and changes that are identified as needed can be changed quickly because there are so few people who have to be in on the decision making process. If the curriculum is out of line, then those few people can quickly realign and get the curriculum going in the right direction.

The problem is, of course, one of time and expertise. These few people are very busy and have no real amount of extra time they can devote to the curricular design process. They do not have the time to do the research and development needed to properly assess and develop their curriculum and still do their full-time teaching jobs. Where in a larger school someone at the central office level would do the ground work to begin the process or perhaps much of the total work and then run by the staff for approval and editing, the rural school teacher may be needed to "do it all." The only answer is to give the staff you do have released time and blocks of it to talk with one another and align the curriculum. This can be done by placing subs in the classrooms and on professional development days if your state still allows them. No matter what you have to do, you must give adequate time and direction to your limited staff to get the curriculum aligned and assessed.

Past Neglect

Harvey Littrell in an article he wrote about rural school and curriculum development listed past neglect as a real issue with curriculum development. Mr. Littrell states in his work that, because curricular development is many times shoved back and not concentrated on, teachers become apathetic about it and do not see the sense of urgency to make an effective change. This is a real problem and must be addressed by the school superintendent.

The curriculum of the school system MUST be a high priority and must continually be reviewed and assessed to be sure it is giving the students an adequate chance to compete with all other students across the state and nation, no matter what the size of the district. To allow staff to use the size and lack of resources as an excuse to not address curricular needs is not acceptable. As the superintendent, you have to be the champion of curricular development, design and assessment. It comes down to this … if you can't get it done, find someone who can. Even if you have to hire an outside consultant to come help get your curriculum aligned with standards and mapped vertically and horizontally, it must happen.

Course Offerings

Anyone who has been a leader at the building level or the central office level in a rural setting understands the difficulty in providing an adequate number of course offerings, especially in middle and secondary schools. The term "singleton" strikes fear into anyone who is trying to develop a schedule for a small school. Of course, this means that there is going to be a course offered, but only one section of it, so all student schedules somehow have to allow for them to be in the one class offered at the one time, thus the "singleton." So, how can the rural school leader offer more classes to the few students that may desire or need the course for their chosen career path? How can multiple foreign languages be offered in a high school where only a fraction of the students even desire a foreign language offering at all? The answer, of course, is to think out of the box and use technology to offer courses in a non-traditional manner. This can be not only foreign languages, but also advanced science courses. Just because the rural school may have limited staff and numbers of students should not thwart an individual student's access to "the good stuff" that larger districts are able to provide. Your job as instructional leader is to find ways to meet the curricular needs of your student—not to find excuses why you can't do it.

Lack of Champions and/or Experts

This is a real issue in the rural setting and not one that should be taken lightly. There is a real resource issue in that there are just not enough people to go around and do all the things that need to be done to meet the needs of the students under your care. Gearld Bailey in another article written about the issues with rural schools and curricular development suggests that the school leader may, in fact, have to hire an outside consultant to aide in the curricular development and assessment. This may sound like blasphemy when suggesting hiring someone to assist. In reality some may say the district cannot afford it, but this author believes you may not be able *not* to afford it! That is not double talk (although it is a double negative), but if the curriculum is not aligned with state and national standards and not properly mapped for the staff to follow, then student needs may not be met. It therefore is imperative if there is not a champion of curricular reform and development available in your rural district, you must go outside and garner the help you need. This need not be an extremely expensive process, and collaborating with nearby universities may be a way to get some help. Any dollars spent should have assessment of success tied to them and those assisting in the process must be held accountable.

Staff Inconsistency

This is an obstacle that will not be overcome in a rural district or any other district for that matter. In a rural district it has much more impact simply because of the lack of numbers. Losing one teacher in the secondary English department can effectively wipe out all or a major portion of the department and, without some sense of curricular alignment and assessment, the department could be starting all over once a replacement has been hired. This is another primary reason the curriculum must be aligned and mapped out so the roadmap for students' success is well laid out no matter who the teacher is. This also allows the new staff member to have a specific guide to know exactly where the students should be, and how they need to take them to the next level in the subject area assigned.

Board Lack of Interest

Most school boards, but especially in a rural setting, will not be experts in the field of educational reform and curricular design. That is the reason they hire the superintendent to be the educational leader of the district. This author has heard the never-ending complaints from sitting district leaders that "the board just doesn't care about curriculum" and therefore it is just hard to get anything done. To that, the response is "get over it." It is not the board's job to lead the curricular development, design and assessment. It is the educational leader's job to do that no matter what it takes. The school board is most often made up of laypeople that love schools and love the children who are in them, but they are not curriculum specialists or experts in the current standards. That is why they hire a professional educator to lead this effort for the benefit of the children in the schools they represent. The responsibility of the district leader is to be sure that the curriculum the school has adopted is aligned with standards and is being taught with best practices so students will learn and be able to compete in an ever-changing society. To do any less would be a disservice to our profession and most especially to the children we have been given the responsibility to serve.

Finally, as we are mapping, aligning and assessing our curricular offerings, if we do not examine the entire curriculum to be sure that our students are gaining insight into the diverse cultural aspects of our community, state, nation and world, we are not finished with our curricular design. After all, as was stated at the beginning, this may be the student's only chance to see the diversity of the world through the eyes of the curriculum you develop.

From the rural school perspective, the superintendent is the curriculum director; the task of developing a curriculum that reflects the diversity of the community, nation, and world falls on his shoulders. A comprehensive understanding and appreciation of a multicultural curriculum is vital. Banks (1999) states that a multicultural curriculum may have four instructional approaches:

1. The Contributions approach utilizes the selection of books, articles, and other resources to celebrate the contributions of people of diversity. Reading about Martin Luther King Jr., for example, during the month of January is part of this approach. However, this approach does not allow diverse material to become recognized as a specific part of the curriculum.

2. The Additive Approach allows the instructor/teacher to actually incorporate literature about and by people of diversity into the curriculum without changing the curriculum. However, this approach simply adds missing material; it does not transform thinking.

3. The Transformational Approach supports changing the structure of the curriculum while encouraging students to view concepts, themes, and problems from the perspective of people of diversity. This approach encourages critical thinking.

4. The Social Action Approach combines the transformational approach with social activities designed to promote social change. This approach provides instruction and encourages students to seek an understanding of social isues and policies while asking why such things happen or if such policies are necessary.

Suburban Perspective

The first requirement of any school wanting to meet the needs of its students (regardless of its level of diversity) is for the teachers to have a comprehensive curriculum. Such a curriculum is not merely a study guide or syllabus of a course, it is not simply a state standard reprinted in a handbook, nor a list of content headings in a course list. A successful and comprehensive curriculum should include at least five key components. It must first define its content or subject matter. For instance, rural life in the 19th Century is a defined content area. Next, the curriculum should make reference to a standard. In our current educational configuration nationally, this will very likely be a specific state standard or a numeric reference to it. This provides a common understanding point for all using the curriculum. The next critical piece of curriculum is a description of what the learner will know or be able to do as it relates to the standard within the content area. This is called a skill and is stated in some form as a verbal action. An example would be, "The student will create and present to the teacher a semantic web." The next part of a successful curriculum is an assessment piece. This should be formative assessment in which the level of student learning is measured. The key to good formative assessment is that it is done frequently on a daily or weekly basis. Finally, the curriculum must have a clear time frame that delineates when throughout the year the teaching and learning described in the skills will occur.

The administrator, in a district leadership position, needs to support the development of this process and allow teachers and the administration at the building level sufficient time to "map" the curriculum. After this mapping process is complete, it should be published and distributed (electronically and in hard copy) to members of the entire school community. The key for the success of the document, after it is done, is that it becomes a highly utilized, ever-evolving document that all teachers at all levels accept and use as their daily guide for instruction. In short, teachers must all be dependent on it for planning and implementing all instruction in their classrooms.

In the real administrator's world, this seemingly simple process is not easily achieved, and due to its ever-evolving nature, it is really a document that will never be fully completed. The reality of mapping a five-pronged curriculum is that in both a diverse and a homogeneous school setting, it is a basic fundamental requirement for positive student achievement and learning.

Once Mapped, Then What?

Once the five-pronged curriculum is mapped and distributed to all the school community, then what? The administrator must next ensure that the teaching staff at all levels is provided training opportunities so they can effectively learn how to differentiate their instruction in the classroom. This author would recommend that Carol Ann Tomlinson's *How to Differentiate Instruction in Mixed-Ability Classrooms* become required reading and a guidebook for all educators in the district. Differentiation is a critical element for successful instruction in a diverse school district in that it will result in the learning needs of each individual student being met, and it will encourage student growth and improvement.

Differentiation is more than just individualized instruction though. Practiced properly in the classroom, it creates multiple ways for learning to occur, and it can motivate students to achieve more effectively than traditional instructional methods. Tomlinson's book (referenced above) provides a practical guide for teachers, showing them how to initiate, implement, and continue those practices of differentiated instruction effectively in the classroom for an extended time.

"Summative assessment just weighs a pig. Formative assessment provides the information you need to feed the pig so it grows" (Wilson, 2008).

Once the curriculum is developed and teachers are using methods involving differentiated instruction in the classroom, there are a few other critical pieces that need to be addressed to ensure that student progress is maintained. The first is that the formative assessment piece of the five-pronged curriculum plan must be used to diagnose students' learning needs. This is a key to an effective curriculum, especially in the diverse student population, because it makes the curriculum meet the need of each individual student and allows them to progress at a realistic and personalized pace toward that learning as a result of data.

Another aspect which has a great deal to do with the successful use of a curriculum and with quality of instruction is the presence of a caring teacher. Stronge summarizes this concept very clearly. "Indeed a hallmark of caring teachers is that they seek to understand the needs, hopes, and aspirations of their students. They know students on an individual basis and demonstrate their concern for both the educational success and personal needs of their students" (Stronge, 2007).

In summary, a five-pronged curriculum developed with teachers, with differentiated instruction, practiced by highly caring teachers, will benefit all students, but especially those with diverse backgrounds. This formula for success is easily stated, but the actual process to get there is much more difficult. The time and commitment required just to get a five-pronged curriculum written is a significant one. The educational leader in a diverse school setting will benefit students significantly by accomplishing it, but it is definitely one of the most difficult challenges he/she will face.

Urban Perspective

Superintendents of urban school districts must fully understand that it is all about academic preparation. Curriculum development and assessment are means to an end. They will allow urban districts to provide the appropriate curriculum and assess its effectiveness based on proven performance of its students. Performance will be evaluated to improve the development and quality of the educational program. Peter Drucker once said, "The effective organization optimizes." Schools that optimize are able to precisely identify their goals and expected outcomes. Urban schools have to work to optimize the instruction of its students.

Curriculum assessment and development requires the proper alignment of curriculum, instruction, and evaluation or assessment. Urban superintendents should ensure the proper educational alignment because today's curricula are inclusive of state standards and expected state tests information. A curriculum is broader than a single textbook, and urban superintendents must insist that the curriculum is being taught in each classroom and school in the district. If the curriculum is taught and the test is aligned with the instruction, urban students will perform as well as suburban students on state assessments. It is simply amazing how smart urban students become when they are taught what they should be covering in the subject and at the appropriate rigor levels.

Academic Freedom or Folly

There are many outstanding teachers in urban schools across this country. Many of them are experts in their subjects and in how to work with diverse student populations. However, there are also a number of urban teachers teaching subjects that they are not certified nor qualified to teach. Too often these subjects are in the shortage areas of math, science, and special education. It is an ongoing challenge for urban superintendents to find certified teachers in the math, science, and special education areas. This is a major concern, but just as serious is the lack of articulation and uniformity in what is being taught to children in the individual classrooms. Many teachers operate or instruct students based upon what they want to teach them. This is a common problem when there is a weak central curriculum department or where districts have decided to decentralize the operations of schools to school-based or site-based decision making. These kinds of schools create a "district of schools," but not a "school district." There is a tremendous difference in the two operations.

District of Schools

A district of schools has a curriculum, but each school has the prerogative to do something different. The textbook adoption choice is a local school decision. The writing style is a local school decision. Selection of the principal and teachers is a local school decision. Maybe they will follow the district calendar, but it is a local school decision. Year-round schools is a local decision as long as students attend the expected number of school days per year. In some decentralized urban situations, they have budget autonomy and are appropriate funds on a formula which is commonly dictated by dollars per average daily membership. Field trips are a local school decision. Promotion or retention is a local school decision. This decentralized operation results in every school doing "its own thing" and having its identity or freedom.

The No Child Left Behind mandates included in state tests and assessments go against this "freedom to be" school operation. There is only one curriculum that aligns with the states assessments, and if these schools are not teaching that curriculum, the students will do poorly on the state tests. However, there are other problems with this "district of schools." One common factor or fact in urban school districts is poverty. Another associated fact is mobility. Poor urban students have high mobility rates. Some students move two or three times in one school semester or approximately every 18 weeks. When they move in and out of schools with school-based autonomy, it is like moving to different school districts. In some schools, their textbooks are different. In other schools, their reading series is different. Some have different styles of writing. At the secondary level, it gets interestingly pathetic. In some schools there are no vocal music programs. Other schools don't have business classes. Other schools don't have advance placement classes or dual credit classes. Other schools don't have weight training classes. Other schools don't teach any social studies electives. This goes on and on. A district of schools sounds like a good idea, but with a diverse, urban and mobile population of students, it is not the best way to ensure educational equity, instructional integrity and programmatic fairness.

A School District

A school district should be just that—a network of schools connected by a common curriculum, which is aligned with classroom instruction and assessment of student performance. A district has common courses with a primary list of adopted textbooks, a defined writing style, reading series, required and elected courses of study. A district has policies and guidelines mandating operations, expectations and practices.

A district should have no problem with the mandates of the No Child Left Behind Law or state testing requirements. The curriculum, instruction and assessments are fully aligned with the state's standards and learning outcomes. Teachers don't have the right or choice to decide what to teach in a school district. The curriculum directs the teacher in what to teach. The teacher has the freedom and choice to decide how to teach the state's standards and curriculum. The *what* is mandated by curriculum; the *how* is determined by the teacher. This is the only way to ensure that children are taught what is required at each grade level in each subject or course.

This seems very simple to understand, but too many urban school districts have problems putting all of this together. There is a strong urge or desire by teachers to teach what they were taught or to teach what they like to teach. One of the other features in the curriculum is the pacing of the curriculum. There are time blocks for each standard or topic to be covered. The social studies teachers do not have the luxury of taking the whole nine weeks on teaching the Civil War in United States history. If this much time is taken on one battle, there is no way to get the students to the war in Iraq by May of the school year. The pacing of teaching is very important. Our country and our textbooks have been accused of attempting to cover too much and to cover it at a very surface level. They say we go "a mile wide and an inch deep." It is true that our textbooks are big and the cost goes with the size, but the textbook is not the curriculum. Teachers cannot be prisoners to textbooks. The curriculum is much broader than a book. The curriculum requires teachers to be experts. It requires teachers to put the lesson together to cover the curriculum. Teachers must use assorted resources and activities to bring the curriculum to life for the students.

After a lesson is taught, students need to demonstrate what they have learned. This is why assessment is so important. Assessment informs instruction of its effectiveness. If students' performance is less than proficient, then the instruction should be reviewed, revised and presented in a more effective manner.

People, the Curriculum and Accountability

Across the country and in many parts of the world, curriculums are very common. There are numerous curriculums for school districts and for individual subjects or courses. There are just as many assessment instruments and processes. The essential key to having an effective curriculum and curriculum assessment and development is the people. Preparation of the people is the fundamental step to the operation. Administrators and teachers should have a solid understanding of the curriculum, the role of textbooks and other resources, the importance of curriculum assessment and how to improve instruction. Building a sense of ownership and accountability is created through participation and involvement.

Curriculum Study Committee

Curriculum study committees are very important. In urban school districts there is a centralized curriculum organization. This is commonly composed of curriculum directors in the core areas. There are also subject specialists and other specialists in the areas of special education, title programs, and special grant programs. These people create a small cadre of curriculum workers. It is common to have these professionals take care of most of the curriculum work, but this is not always the best process for involving building administrators and subject area teachers. Creating subject area building activities and having one or two building representatives to participate on a district curriculum study committee in each subject area creates greater ownership and accountability. The curriculum study committee meets no more than four times per school year, but these meetings create a districtwide curriculum relationship. The agenda for these meetings is very important. Issues like end-of-course assessments, effective teaching practices, use of technology in teaching the subject, textbook issues and concerns, curriculum evaluation and assessment, prioritizing state standards, and other instructional and program issues can all be scheduled over the school year.

The value of curriculum study committees is in the awareness and understanding it provides to administrators and teachers. Urban school districts need this kind of committee to reduce the impersonal nature of large centralized curriculum structures.

Supervision of Curriculum and Instruction

The primary purpose of a solid curriculum and curriculum assessment and development is to provide the best educational instruction program for students. However, having all of this is just half of the answer. The critical half is the instruction in the classroom. The classroom teachers are the most valuable piece of the educational process. Teachers are expected to be experts in their subject areas and have the skills and ability to effectively teach their students. It is a very challenging and demanding job. However, administrative supervision of classroom teaching is the key to ensuring a quality level of teaching. If school principals and other administrators use the teacher evaluation process; walk-through practices; pre-observation, observation and post-observation instructional procedures; they will be able to help teachers do their best work.

Administrators have to take a personal sense of accountability for ensuring quality teaching for students. An essential starting point is demanding that each teacher really is teaching. If new teachers or beginning teachers are not prepared to successfully instruct and supervise students, they should not be allowed to continue to teach a second year. This is especially true in urban school districts. Urban students bring many gaps and deprivations to school. They require the best possible instruction, remediation and supplemental services. They respond to active, engaging, direct and hands-on instruction. Urban superintendents must set the focus on academic rigor. Too many citizens and patrons have low expectations of urban students, but administrators and teachers must know that the key to student performance is the quality of the teaching and support activities given them. Schools and teaching do make a difference in the success of the students and this point is essential in urban school districts. Diversity does not mean deficiency. It is very powerful and requires the best teaching possible. Everything should be focused on providing the best classroom for instructing urban children. This should be the driving force behind urban district operations.

Chapter 8 Case Studies

Case Study 1: Rural

You have just accepted a position as superintendent of a rural Okla-homa school system of less than 1,000 students. It is a stable community made up of primarily ranches and one small town. You have one elemen-tary and one 7-12 secondary school. It is evident there has been little cur-ricular work completed over the past several years. What are the first five steps you will take on the path to curricular reform for the district based on the information you gained from this chapter?

Case Study 2: Suburban

Your district has always recognized and observed Black History Month. During that time all schools emphasize the African American heritage and history. The district, however, has had a large increase in the Hispanic population and you are approached by an influential member of the Hispanic community and asked why their heritage is not discussed or celebrated and why the curriculum in all subjects shows no signs of meet-ing the diverse needs of his community members. He has talked to some of your building leaders and has become frustrated because he feels they are not taking his concerns seriously. How will you handle this situation?

Case Study 3: Urban

This urban school district has taken a great deal of pride in its school-based decision making operations. Each school has the autonomy to make decisions on personnel employment, curriculum options, transportation options, extra- and co-curricula options and limited financial operations.

However, this school district has the worst or lowest scores on the annual state tests and the school district has failed to make Adequate Yearly Progress (AYP) for the last five years. The state is threatening to take control of the school district. The superintendent has been terminated and you have been selected as the new superintendent. In checking the district performance, you learn that no school at any level is required to follow the state mandated curriculum. Teachers have been allowed to teach the materials they wanted to teach and to take the amount of time they desire to teach each topic. The Teacher-Board Master Contract gives teachers the right to teach what they want to teach and how and when they want to teach it. It is called their "Professional Freedom to Work" law or article. As the new superintendent with the mandate to improve academic rigor and performance on state tests, what will you do to get the job done?

Works Cited

Annual Report, Diversity Committee of the College of Liberal Arts and Sciences. 2004, January. Iowa State University. Retrieved 16 May 2008 from the World Wide Web. http://www.las.instate.edu/diversity.

Banks, J. A. 1999. *An Introduction to Multicultural Education.* Boston: Allyn and Bacon.

Covey, Stephen, R. 1990. *The 7 Habits of Highly Effective People.* New York: Simon and Schuster.

Finn, Patrick J. *Literacy With an Attitude 10th Edition.* City Sunny Press: January 2009.

Fullan, Michael. 2001. *Leading a Culture of Change.* Jossey-Bass.

Gollnick, D., & Chin. P. 2006. *Multicultural Education in a Pluralistic Society.* Upper Saddle River. New Jersey: Pearson Education.

Greenleaf, R. 2003. *The Servant Leader Within.* New York: Paulist Press.

Hoover-Dempsey, K., & Sandler, H. 1995. Why Do Parents Become Involved in Their Children's Education. *Review of Education Research. 67.* 3-42.

Kotter, John 1996. *Leading Change.* Boston: Harvard Business School Press.

Kotter, John 2008. *Sense of Urgency.* Boston: Harvard Business School Press.

Kuykendall, C. 1992. *From Rage to Hope: Strategies For Reclaiming Black and Hispanic Students.* Bloomington, Indiana: National Education Service.

Lewis, Larry. 2004. *Unlocking Some of the Endless Doors of Oklahoma School Finance*. Oklahoma State School Board Association Publication. 65-68.

Manning, M., & Baruth, L. 2000. *Multicultural Education of Children and Adolescents*. Boston: Boston, Allyn & Bacon.

Maxwell, J. C. 2002. *The 21 Irrefutable Laws of Leadership*. Nashville: Maxwell Motivation Inc.

National Center for Education Statistics. 2003a. The condition of education 2003 in brief. U.S. Department of Education: Institute of Education Sciences. Retrieved June26, 2006, from http://nces.ed.gov/pubs2003/2003068.pdf.

National Center for Education Statistics. 2003b. Overview of public elementary and secondary schools and districts: School year 2001-02: Statistical analysis report. Washington DC: Lee McGraw Hoffman. Retrieved June 26, 2006, from http://nces.ed.gov/pubs2003/2003411.pdf.

National Center for Education Statistics. 2004. The conditions of education 2004 in brief. U.S. Department of Education: Institute of Education Science. Retrieved June 26, 2006, from http://nces.ed.gov/pubs2004/2004076.pdf.

National Center for Education Statistics. 2005. The conditions of education 2005 in brief. U.S. Department of Education: Institute of Education Science. Retrieved June 26, 2006, from http://nces.ed.gov/pubs2005/2005095.pdf.

National Center for Education Statistics. 2006. The conditions of education 2006 in brief. U.S. Department of Education: Institute of Education Science. Retrieved June 26, 2006, from http://nces.ed.gov/pubs2006/2006072.pdf.

National Education Association. August 2003. Status of the American
    public school Teacher, 2000-2001. Washington, DC: NEA
    RESEARCH. Retrieved June 26, 2006, from
    http://www.nea.org/edstats/images/status.pdf.

Pearse, Robert F. 1972. The Effects of an Executive's Leadership Style
    on His Time Management Practices. Boston: Mimeo.

Pew Hispanic Center. November 11, 2005. The high school Hispanics
    attend: Size and other key characteristics. Retrieved June 28, 2007,
    from http://pewhispanic.org/files/reports54.pdf.

Schein, E. 1999. *The Corporate Culture Survival Guide. :* Jossey-Bass.

Trickett, Joseph M. Summer 1962. A More Effective Use of Time.
    California Management Review.

U.S. Census. 2003. School enrollment: 2000: Census 2000 brief.
    Retrieved June 27, 2006, from
    http://www.census.gov/prod/2003pubs/c2kbr-26.pdf.

Wilkes, C. G. 1998. *Jesus On Leadership.* Wheaton, Illinois: Tyndale
    House.

Wilson, Ray 2008. *Diagnostic Testing.* District Administrator, March
    2008.

Dr. Eugene G. White

Dr. White is the Superintendent of the Indianapolis Public Schools, Indianapolis, Indiana. He is the Past President of the American Association of School Administrators; Past President of the North Central Association of Schools and Colleges; Past President of the Indiana Association of Public School Superintendents.

Dr. White was the first African American High School Principal in the Fort Wayne Community Schools and in the Metropolitan School District of Washington Township's North Central High School. He was the first African American Superintendent of the Metropolitan School District of Washington Township. He was the first African American President of the Indiana Association of Public School Superintendents (IAPSS). Dr. White has authored another book for Colleagues and Practitioners titled *Leadership Beyond Excuses: The Courage to Hold the Rope.*

Wilmer Earl Cooper

Wilmer Cooper has ten years experience as a public school superintendent and has a reputation for outstanding organizational leadership that promotes best practices in administration, supervision and instruction. He came from seven years of experience as a public school secondary principal with service in both rural and metropolitan schools. His extensive background lending support and developing rapport with students from diverse socio-economic and cultural populations make him a natural selection for one of the authors for this text. He has been recognized as a creative and intuitive problem solver who cheerfully overcomes challenges including funding cutbacks, staffing, equipment shortages, classroom overcrowding, and increasing the parental involvement in the schools he serves.

Mr. Cooper has his undergraduate degree and one Masters from Southwestern State University, another Masters degree in Educational Administration from East Central State University and is presently a Doctoral Candidate at Oral Roberts University in Tulsa, Oklahoma.

Dr. Kevin Caress

Dr. Caress has served school corporations in Indiana as teacher, principal and superintendent. He recently accepted a new position as Superintendent of Clark Pleasant Schools after a successful tenure at Frankfort Community Schools. He also has served in various capacities at Indiana University while working towards his doctorate degree. During his undergraduate years he spent one year abroad studying at Universidad de Sevilla in Seville, Spain. Kevin is fluent in Spanish which has been a very valuable asset while leading the Frankfort Schools. During his tenure as Superintendent the community experienced a large increase in the Hispanic population and Kevin's ability to speak the native language became an invaluable tool for meeting the needs of his diverse student population.

Dr. Caress is a member of Association for Supervision and Curriculum Development (ASCD), Phi Delta Kappa, Indiana Association of Public School Superintendents and The American Association of School Administrators (ASSA).

Printed in the United States
148814LV00004B/1/P